Anxiety in Relationships

How to Eliminate Panic Attacks, Insecurity, and Jealousy in Love. Discover the Secrets of Improved Communication to Avoid Couple's Conflict and Narcissistic Relationships

D1716354

Written by **Theresa Williams**

Table of Contents

ANXIETY IN RELATIONSHIPS
THERESA WILLIAMS

"Never lose hope.
Good things will come soon"

THERESA WILLIAMS

Introduction

Being in a relationship, especially with someone special, and experiencing anxiety issues (or having an anxiety disorder) can be very depressing. Often, you may get the impression that anxiety is like having a third person in the relationship, an imaginary personality that comes in between you and your partner. This anxiety is responsible for all the confusion and issues you experience in your relationship.

Anxiety can cause periods of panic, feelings of fear, or a sense of being overwhelmed, uneasy, or tense. Anxiety can take over your thoughts, spread into many other areas of your life, and can thereby affect your reasoning and productivity. It infuses a strain in relationships and puts them at great risk. When anxiety is thriving in a relationship, the trust and connection that every relationship need is broken. When anxiety sets in, it takes your mind off the most important aspects of your relationship, and you become less attuned to the needs and desires of your partner. Fear and worry become the order of the day.

You feel overwhelmed and worried about what is happening but find it difficult to pay attention to what is happening. When this occurs, your partner may feel as though you are not present. When you are anxious in your relationship, you may find it difficult to express your true feelings. If you don't express what you truly feel or need, anxiety becomes more intense, and your emotions will begin to run out of control if you keep bottling them in. This leads to you feeling overwhelmed and defensive.

Intimate relationships can reflect the best and worst of us all. They are mirrors that can fuel our struggles or calm them. Anxiety is a poison that can steal the joy and connection between two people who belong together. Perhaps you have been with your partner for a long time, yet you constantly wrestle with the notion that your partner doesn't live up to your expectations and will not be able to fill that void in your heart.

Maybe you also suspect that you are part of the problem. Perhaps you are insecure in love; you feel lonely and desire a companion and lover to accompany you through the adventure and journey of life. You constantly wonder if anyone would be truly there for you if you let down your guard and are yourself. Would you be able to find comfort, reassurance, and support from them in your vulnerability? You ponder over these things at every opportunity.

Many people can face their fears and overcome every anxiety and limiting force, blocking their joy. This is not only for couples or romantic partners; it is also for singles that look forward to a wholesome and healthy relationship.

This guide contains practical strategies and exercises that you can use to help you with your growth and healing journey.

When you consciously implement all that has been written and take all the exercises to heart, you will have conquered a large part of the anxiety that ruins your relationships. You will begin to feel less insecure and attached in love. By reading, you will be able to identify irrational behaviors that trigger anxiety and take concrete and positive steps to eliminate those behaviors.

I want you to know that you can enjoy a healthy, wholesome, and valuable love life, a relationship in which you are not needy and don't feel insecure or attached. You can have a loving relationship in which you see yourself growing and adding positive value to your partner.

You will understand your relationship struggles as you flip through the pages; this is the perfect opportunity for you to discover your potential. You are worthy of great love, valuable love, quality, and everlasting love—a love so true and pure, it will stand the test of time. You will be able to identify the obstacles to nurturing happy relationships, and how to avoid these obstacles. Through self-awareness, you will be able to develop a more secure and intimate relationship with your partner and lover.

This book will also help you ignite your love life and keep your heart and mind full of love, peace, security, and value. Make the most of it all, take your time to read it, make notes as you read each page, and treat it as a guide. Commit all the exercises and strategies to heart. You will surely see positive changes in your relationships if you put your all into conquering anxiety. Keep a journal to document your thoughts as you read and write down your next course of action for your relationships. Let's get started and good luck on your journey to a better life!

CHAPTER 1

"Overview of anxiety"

Chapter 1: Overview of Anxiety
What Is Anxiety?

When someone suffers from an anxiety disorder, they frequently feel an emotion characterized by physical symptoms, feelings of tension, and worried thoughts. These symptoms are different from the "normal" feelings of anxiety we experience, as they typically linger, and, when left unchecked or untreated, can start significantly affecting our lives. Therefore, if your partner suffers from anxiety, it's important to understand the condition and know how to help them manage it.

People who suffer from an anxiety disorder may experience anxious feelings all the time, no matter what situation they are in. These feelings are intense and can be debilitating, causing a person to lose interest in their life or the things they enjoy. In the most extreme cases, a person who suffers from anxiety might not even want to leave their home because of these feelings. If this condition isn't treated, or if the person doesn't learn how to manage their symptoms, it will just keep getting worse over time.

Anxiety disorders are a type of emotional condition, and these can affect anyone. Women have a higher likelihood of developing this condition and being diagnosed with it than men do. While there are different types of anxiety disorders, all of them share some common symptoms, including:

- Always feeling "on-edge"

- Uncontrollable feelings of restlessness, irritability, and worry

- Difficulty concentrating

- Not being able to fall asleep or stay asleep throughout the night

While everyone may experience some of these symptoms occasionally, for those who suffer from anxiety, these symptoms are a normal part of life for them. Imagine how difficult it is to have to experience these symptoms all the time. Naturally, if you have anxiety, you might start taking it out on the people closest to you, especially if things get to be too much. Therefore, it's important to learn about anxiety if your partner suffers from it—so that your relationship won't be destroyed by it.

There is no single test that can diagnose this condition. Instead, the person needs to undergo a long and comprehensive process that involves psychological questionnaires, physical examinations, and evaluations of mental health. Some doctors even request urine or blood tests to make sure that the person isn't suffering from any other underlying medical condition that may be causing the symptoms. If your partner seems to be suffering from anxiety, you may suggest that they consult with a doctor to get a proper diagnosis. After all, it's always better to be sure so that you can start helping your partner recover from their condition, or at least learn how to manage it together.

Normal Feelings of Anxiety vs. Unhealthy Anxiety

Anxiety is a normal emotion, and it can often be healthy. Normal feelings of anxiety are essential for our survival. We feel anxious in the face of threats or danger, allowing us to react appropriately. This anxiety causes an adrenaline rush in our bodies, which in turn, activates our body's "fight-or-flight" response. This physiological reaction prepares you to either flee from the situation or confront it. When a person always feels anxiety at disproportionate levels, this may indicate that they are suffering from some type of anxiety disorder. Being in a relationship with a person who suffers from anxiety can be extremely frustrating, especially if you don't know how to handle it. If your partner doesn't know how to handle their condition either, this can spell the end of your relationship. For people who suffer from unhealthy anxiety, the severity or duration of their anxious feelings are typically out of proportion to the stressor or trigger that causes them. Then they may start experiencing physical symptoms, like nausea and an increase in blood pressure, which in turn, might increase their feelings of anxiety. When a person's anxiety develops into a disorder, it can start interfering with their life. To help you understand the difference between normal anxiety and unhealthy anxiety, let's go through some of the key differences:

1. Condition

Normal anxiety fades away after the trigger or stressor goes away. However, for those struggling with anxiety disorders, the condition affects all aspects of their life. It starts taking a toll on their health, cripples their ability to accomplish tasks, and takes away the joy of living. Most people who suffer from this condition resort to avoidance, which, sadly, can be very debilitating on its own. In the case of your relationship, your partner might even start avoiding you when things get bad.

2. Length and Intensity

Normal anxiety is a fleeting emotion that doesn't last long, and its intensity depends on the severity of the situation. However, when it comes to unhealthy anxiety, the person could experience excessive and intense emotional responses for an extended period. Typically, these feelings are disproportionate to the trigger or stressor. For instance, if you get into a fight with your partner, you might feel anxious about it. After some time, those feelings will fade away. Your partner might even continue feeling anxious about it, even after you've made up.

3. Stressor

It's normal to feel some anxiety when a specific trigger or stressor causes that fight-or-flight reaction. However, for those who suffer from anxiety disorders, they may feel anxious even if nothing has triggered them or experience severe anxiety symptoms despite a very small or minimal trigger.

4. Other Symptoms

When you experience normal anxiety, typically, you won't experience any other symptoms. However, unhealthy anxiety comes with other symptoms like a racing heart, trembling, dizziness, nausea, negative thoughts, and more. These symptoms tend to linger if the person feels anxious.

What Is Anxiety in Relationships?

Nearly every facet of a relationship is affected by anxiety, no matter what type. When someone enters a relationship, there are relatively simple expectations that go along with it. First, you assume the other person can fulfill the role of a partner. Being a partner involves a solid ability to communicate openly, offer companionship, contribute financially, hold on to a stable job, and eventually raise a family.

How to Overcome Fear of Loving

Since we have learned that fear is only in the mind and is learned, for nobody was born with it, this means it can also be unlearned. Just like if you learn how to make cars, you must also understand how to destroy them. You must always learn to face your fears so that you can face them. We are going to look at how people can overcome their fears.

Identify Your Fear

Get a grip on what frightens you. Peruse your mind for the ideas or pictures that give you fear. Think through them slowly, comprehend them well, and understand why you are afraid of them.

Be able to observe yourself internally. Without knowing your fear, it will be impossible to overcome it.

Just like in mathematics, while solving the problems, you start with the known to calculate the unknown. Starting with the known is a way of also solving the problems in your mind. In overcoming fear, it is not any different. Identifying your fear is a way of overcoming your fear because it will help you deal with it.

Create Awareness

People are often in denial. Before you can overcome your fear, you must first accept that you are afraid and that it is affecting your health. Sometimes, someone is comfortable with the fear in them, thinking it is meant to be a part of them; in reality, this is wrong. No one is meant to be comfortable with fear. You and fear are two separate things, which is why you can learn to handle it.

Utilize Some Peer Pressure

You are afraid that your partner will not approve something that you are doing, so you decide to let it go. Imagine if you sat with the carefree types—the people that will push you to go ahead and say or do anything without a second thought. It will help you overcome your fears if you can remember any incident in your life that you did not want to do but ended up doing because your friends were doing it. For example, imagine a child who thinks his mother doesn't like seeing him playing guitar. The child is always thinking about playing the guitar. Some of his friends play the guitar without caring whether their parents like it or not. After some time, he develops the courage to tell his mother that he wants to play the guitar. To his surprise, he gets his guitar. Therefore, it was just fear in the mind of the boy, but he was able to overcome it due to peer pressure convincing him to tell his parents he wanted to play.

Get Curious

People have said curiosity causes problems, but when it comes to fear, curiosity can be helpful. You must be curious. Get curious and understand what is causing your fears, how you are reacting to the fears, and how you feel when engulfed by the fear. Finally, observe yourself and understand what is going on deep within you.

Gratitude

When you feel your fear overwhelming you, start thinking about what you are grateful for. If you are afraid of loving him, be grateful that he came for you instead of the many others out there.

Writing or Journaling

Just as we discussed writing down the issues going on in your mind, you should also write down your fears. Write down your fears and face them one by one because if you start thinking about them, you will find yourself thinking endlessly without a solution to any of them. You have to write them down to gain a sense of proportion and significance. How big are they? How many are there? Do they deserve your attention or not?

Sometimes you might be thinking that it is big, and since you do not know how to go about it, you overthink and see a big giant that you do not dare face. Writing them down will help you narrow the list of things you want to do. It is a way of overcoming fear.

For example, you need makeup that you will use before you go to a party. You do not know which makeup you want, so you start thinking about makeups. You think of all the types you know; you overthink about it until you are so confused and afraid that none of them might make you look good at the party.

But what if you wrote down a list of the makeup you need for the party. It would be easier, it will save you time, and there won't be any stress or fear that applying it won't make you pretty. This is the same as writing down your fears. Write them down, and then handle them squarely.

Open Up

Opening is about revealing and talking about your fears. Find someone that will listen and talk to them. Hopefully, they can advise you on what to do. Open to your partner in the relationship. Who knows, maybe what you fear is something that does not bother your partner at all, and they can help you sort it out.

Therapy

Nowadays, there are many psychological resources. Find a professional, open, cry if needed, and pour your heart out. A therapist will help you understand how to overcome your fear. Find someone that you feel comfortable with, that you trust, and will be helpful for your situation. In this case, attitude matters.

Persistence

They say that insanity is when you do the same thing repeatedly hoping for a new result. When you try to overcome fear, be persistent; do it again and again but in a different way. The first time you do it, if it does not work, change the strategy, and try again. Do not give up along the way. Overcoming fear is a process, and just like any process, there is no single step for success. There must be a variety of steps, and persistence through the entire process, for it to be successful.

Change Your Attitude

If your attitude towards the fear you are overcoming is wrong, then it will give you a headache trying to overcome it. Move forward with a positive attitude, believe it is possible to handle it, and believe you are going to handle it; this is the way to conquer your fear.

Research

Do comprehensive research on your issues. Read case studies about your fear and understand how they were handled. This can help you find a solution to your fears.

Act

Trust in yourself. Believe that these are just fears, you are a fighter, and you can get past the fears. Tell yourself that these are just creations of your imagination, designed to scare you, so face them. If you are afraid that you are with the wrong person, face the fear. Find out why you think so and why you are afraid that he is not the one. Once you do, you will realize that the fears have become weaker and soon they will leave.

Avoid the 'What If'

If you keep on playing the game of what if, it will send you to an endless pit. The what-if questions mostly focus on the negative rather than on the positive. Stay positive. Sometimes you may find yourself asking questions like, what if he thinks I am weak? and What if he does not like my ideas? What if he becomes angry when I do not do this for him? So many questions pile up in your head and end up mounting to so many fears that will steal the happiness out of your life completely.

It will do you good to overcome your fears by changing your what-ifs. For example, think of what will happen the next time he says he loves you. What will happen the next time he smiles at the ideas you have and puts them into action? You have to maintain your positivity. Bury the 'what if' game and you will be able to overcome your fears.

Eat a Balanced Diet

Sometimes the foods we eat activate the fears we have. Sweet sugary meals activate a lot of unhealthy things in our bodies. Stick to a balanced diet and it will help you. Some meals relax the mind and help fight the fears; identify them and stick to them.

Stay Positive

This is a good way of overcoming fear. Instead of being a pessimist, be an optimist. When fear grips you, think of something positive rather than negative. This will help you a great deal when it comes to fighting your fears.

Surrender

There is no need to fight a losing battle. Sometimes you fight your fears until you feel completely exhausted. Instead of continuing to fight, let them in. What does not kill you makes you stronger. Let your fears make you stronger. Stop fighting.

Give Up Control

Most of the time, we are afraid of losing relationships, so we tend to want to control every move and every step of the journey of love. When we mess up just a little bit, we hate ourselves. Just like letting go or surrendering to anything else, let go of the control. Allow yourself to make mistakes. You don't always have to be in control. Let go of the control.

CHAPTER 2

"Phases of a relationship and reasons for the conflicts"

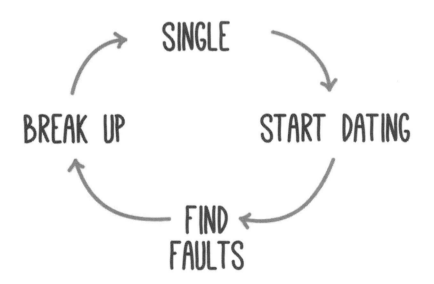

Chapter 2: Phases of a Relationship and Reasons for Conflicts

Marriage is often idealized by believing it is a static form that must remain identical over the years. Still, marriage is a process, not a given condition! Sometimes, partners only worry that their relationship stays intact, rather than face any conflicts and inevitable evolution.

As preparation for marriage, it is important to accept the idea that each stage of development involves crises that are typical and normal. We must adequately overcome these crises to keep the union alive. Indeed, it is not the emergence of the crises that is pathological; it is the attempt to avoid them, which are normal in themselves.

By bonding with a partner, you are looking for temporary satisfaction or confirmation. Still, you want to build your life together, engage in a common path, build your home, start a family, and find your lifestyle. Forming a stable relationship as a couple requires an exclusive character, not only in front of other possible partners, but also for the family. By building one's own family, the process of identification and autonomy is concluded.

In the life cycle of a couple, we can hypothesize different evolutionary phases, as E. Bader and P. Pearson writes in their manual. The couple initially goes through the phases of symbiosis, differentiation, experimentation, rapprochement, and mutual interdependence. Evolution does not always succeed in completing itself, and this results in the onset of painful problems or the breakdown of the relationship.

Let's briefly look at each of these stages:

1) **Bonding:** This is the phase of the so-called "falling in love" process, in which there is a very strong idealization of the other. As lovers, only the similarities are perceived; the differences are canceled. More trust is attributed to the other than to oneself; the satisfaction of someone's needs is delegated to the other.

2) **Differentiation:** This is the stage following the symbiotic one in the evolution of the couple. The differentiation is a consequence of the disappointment that the other is not the idealized figure created in the phase of falling in love. This phase is also called the "awakening" and arouses contradictory feelings. On the one hand, it is disappointing to note the differences and disagreements. However, it can become rewarding and stimulating to discover the other person in his or her uniqueness.

   Indeed, a couple evolves from the symbiotic state to that of differentiation when it begins to think independently, and there is a shift towards introspection. The difficulties become more intense when one of the two is not ready and puts in place all attempts to maintain the symbiosis's status quo. In this case, the change is seen as a signal of pathological deterioration of the relationship, rather than a natural evolutionary process.

3) **Practicing:** In this phase of the couple's life cycle, it is very difficult to compromise and negotiate, because there is emotional detachment. The salient feature of this phase is "distance." The

couple is competitive, and there is no empathy. It is the stage where "me" prevails. Any one partner wants to give up, fights, and argues peacefully, and there is no emotional connection. It is important, at this stage, to be able to take responsibility for your anger toward your partner.

4) **Rapprochement and synergy:** A new relational contract is quite different from the symbiotic one. We return to the partner to resolve the conflicts together. The two elements of the couple are independent, but at the same time, they are able and want to help others. This is the phase where it turns out that the defect of the other makes you smile. If the two argue, they do it based on the contents and not on the person.

The generalized anxiety disorder (GAD) can hurt several aspects of your life, including your relationships.

These are some of the specific ways that your distress can lead to problems maintaining relationships with others. The techniques can be implemented (under the guidance of a specialist in mental health) to help you manage their unhealthy attachments.

Being Dependent

Many people with GAD hold their partners (or friends) closely and continually rely on them for reassurance.

Fighting Problem-based Dependency

When you develop overly dependent relationships, find ways to cope, and rely more on yourself to feel better, your partner or friend can be put under pressure.

For example, if you are angry or suspicious about these relationships, you should first note that your anxiety could fuel it. Nevertheless, take some time to think about any hard data (facts) that will help your interest in trying to gain insight.

A therapist specializing in talk therapy, called cognitive behavioral therapy, can help you formulate strategies to reassure you and act on your own rather than needing the comfort of your partner whenever you are anxious.

Treating Your Anxiety and Relationship Problems

A therapist will explore the impact of GAD on your relationships. Exploring the feelings more closely, for example, can be a good strategy for someone who tends to avoid relationships. On the other hand, this strategy can backfire on people who are more emotionally reactive and reliant on others.

Be sure that you can develop healthy, long-term, and fulfilling relationships with others with the proper treatment.

Anxiety-Filled Conversation

Whether you ask, or deduce it after months of dating, there will be a point when your partner discloses his or her anxiety. It's a crucial moment in the relationship, so be sensitive and do not judge. Thank them for trusting you with the information. They most likely have not shared this with many people. See it as the beginning of a discussion that will resurface occasionally.

How Anxiety May Affect Your Relationship

Your partner probably spends a lot of time worrying and ruminating about everything that may go wrong or has already gone wrong. Listed below are some examples of thoughts and questions that may be on the mind of your partner:

- What if he doesn't love me as much as I love him?

- What if he's hiding something from me?

- What if she is lying to me?

- What if he's going to cheat me?

- What if she likes someone else better?

- What if we break up?

- What if he ghosts on me?

- What if he doesn't reply to my messages?

- What if my anxiety ruins our relationship?

- What if I am only the first to reach out?

Most people have at least some of these worrying thoughts. They are a normal part of a relationship, particularly a new one. However, people with anxiety problems or an anxiety disorder tend to have these anxious thoughts more frequently and more intensely.

"Our thoughts are taking over and heading straight into the worst-case scenario," said Michelene Wasil, a therapist who understands both personal and psychiatric anxiety.

Anxiety causes physiological effects, including shortness of breath and sleeplessness. Anxious people can react to stress with the fight-or-flight response as if the stress is a physical attack.

Sometimes, distressing thoughts motivate your partner to act in ways that stress the relationship. For example, psychologist Jennifer B. Rhodes said, "People with anxiety often check their partner's involvement with insecure approaches." These strategies usually address one of their anxious convictions.

ANXIETY IN RELATIONSHIPS
THERESA WILLIAMS

CHAPTER 3

"Getting over relationship insecurity"

Chapter 3: Getting Over Relationship Insecurity

Codependency (Relationship Addiction)

An unhealthy reliance on other people for acceptance and a sense of identity are among the core features of codependency. The word is less analytical, individually, and more descriptive of a complex relationship.

A codependent relationship, in its simplest terms, is when one partner needs the other partner, who needs to be needed in turn. This circular relation is the basis of what experts refer to when they define the codependency "loop."

The self-esteem and self-worth of the codependent will only come from sacrificing themselves for their mate, who is only too glad to accept their sacrifices.

Codependency Fast Facts:

- Codependent relationships may be among friends, romantic partners, or family members.

- Sometimes, emotional, or physical violence is part of the relationship.

- Friends and family members of a co-dependent individual may believe that something is wrong.

- As with any mental or emotional health problem, care requires time, commitment, and the assistance of a clinician.

Codependence vs. Dependency

With codependence, one person prioritizes their needs over the needs of the other.

Knowing the difference between being dependent on another person—which can be a positive and beneficial trait—and being detrimental to codependency is crucial.

Below are some examples that explain the difference:

Dependent: For support and affection, two people rely on each other. In the relationship, both find value.

Codependent: The codependent individual feels useless because they are needed by the enabler and make drastic sacrifices for it. The enabler gets the satisfaction that the other person meets their every need.

The codependent is only satisfied when their partner makes serious sacrifices. They feel this other person has to need them to have some meaning.

Dependent: Both parties prioritize their relationship, but may find pleasure in external interests, other mates, and hobbies.

Codependent: The codependent has no real identity, goals, or beliefs beyond their relationship of codependence.

Dependent: Both parties should communicate their feelings, desires and find ways for both to make the relationship beneficial.

Codependent: One person feels unimportant and does not express their desires and needs. They might have difficulty knowing anything about their thoughts or needs.

Codependence can be between one or both parties. A codependent individual may overlook other important areas of their lives to satisfy their partner. From their intense commitment to this, one person will damage their everyday obligations in other relationships. The position of an enabler is often unstable. An individual relying on a codependent does not know how to have an equal two-sided relationship, and therefore comes to rely on the sacrifices and needs of another individual.

Codependence Symptoms

It can be difficult to differentiate between a codependent person and one who is only clingy or enamored with someone else. Typically, a person who is codependent will:

1) Find no joy or pleasure in life other than doing things for the other person.

2) Stay in the relationship when they know their partner is doing hurtful things.

3) Do whatever you want to please and fulfill your enabler, no matter what the cost to them.

4) Feel intense uncertainty about their relationship because they still wish to make the other person happy.

5) Using all their time and resources to give everything their partner asks for.

6) Feel guilty in the relationship of talking about them, and do not express any personal wishes or desires.

7) Ignore the other person's values or morality for doing what he wants.

Other people may try to address their problems with the codependent. Even though others say the person is too dependent, it would be difficult for a person in a codependent relationship to leave the relationship.

The codependent person may feel intense conflict about removing himself from the enabler because his own identity depends on sacrificing himself for the other person.

What is the nature of a codependent relationship?

Codependency is an acquired trait that typically stems from past behavioral habits and emotional problems. It was once thought to be the result of living with an alcoholic parent.

Researchers now claim that codependency can come from many circumstances, some of which include substance abuse or mental illness.

Undermining Parental Relationships

Alcohol, narcotics, and other substance addictions are common factors that cause parents to prioritize their needs over their children. This environment may trigger the children to become codependent adults.

Those who are codependent as adults often have issues with their infant or teenage parental relationships. They may have been told that their own needs were less important than the needs of their parents, or not at all relevant. In these families, the child can be taught to concentrate on the needs of the parent and never worry about himself.

Needy parents will tell their children that if they want something for themselves, then they are being selfish or greedy. As a result, the child learns to neglect his or her own needs and thinks, instead, about what they can still do for others.

In these circumstances, one of the parents may have an alcohol or drug abuse problem, a lack of maturity, and emotional growth, resulting in a focus only on their own self-centered needs. These conditions trigger differences in the child's emotional growth, causing them to pursue codependent relationships later.

Living With a Family Member Who Is Mentally or Physically Ill

Codependency can also arise from caring for a person who is chronically ill. Being in the caregiver role, particularly at a young age, may lead the young person to neglect their own needs and develop a habit of only helping others. The self-worth of a person can be built around being wanted by another person and getting nothing in return.

Most people with a sick family member are not codependent. Nonetheless, it may occur in these family environments, especially if the child's parent or caregiver exhibits any of the dysfunctional behaviors mentioned.

Physical, Mental, and Sexual Abuse in Families May Cause Psychological Issues That Last Years or Even a Lifetime.

Codependency is one of the many problems that may emerge from past violence. An abused child or adolescent may learn to repress his or her emotions as a defense mechanism against the pain of violence. As an adult, this learned pattern leads to only thinking about the feelings of others and not understanding their own needs.

Often, an abused person will only seek out abusive relationships, as they are only familiar with this type of relationship. Through codependent relationships, this also manifests itself.

Treatment

Therapy can be more effective in an individual or group setting, compared to couple's therapy. It allows the person to discuss their emotions and actions outside of the relationship.

Many factors may help to shape a positive, healthy relationship. People in codependent relationships will need to take small steps in the relationship toward some separation. They may need to pursue an enjoyable activity or hobby outside the relationship.

A codependent person will seek to spend time with family members or friends who support him. The enabler must realize that by encouraging them to make drastic sacrifices, they are not supporting their codependent partner.

Individual or group counseling is a great benefit to people in codependent relationships. A specialist may assist them in seeking ways to understand and communicate their emotions, which may have been hidden since childhood. People who have been abused will have to accept past trauma and start expressing their feelings and desires again.

Eventually, all partners must learn to identify common behavior patterns in a codependent relationship, such as "needing to be wanted" and requiring the other individual to center their lives on them.

Taking such measures may not be easy but are worth the effort to help both parties learn how to be in a two-sided and respectful relationship.

How Your Insecurities Make Your Relationship Insecure

The bottom line is that you need to have some degree of confidence in your relationship for it to run smoothly. If you're feeling insecure, your relationship with your partner is likely to suffer. Both people must be communicative and open in a relationship, or the relationship will start to crumble. Accordingly, when insecurity rears its head, couples are less likely to be honest with one another, which will only further the seed of doubt that has been planted in the relationship. Stop this seed before it grows into something much bigger than you, or your partner can control. The more you neglect the insecurities, the more difficult it will be to salvage the relationship.

Insecurity inevitably gives you anxiety. When you feel insecure, you can't help but focus too much attention on your insecurity than it deserves. You become obsessed with something that other people often don't even notice because insecurity is often just us being too self-critical. It is nitpicking our qualities and traits and unfairly judging ourselves based on those things. Everyone has insecurities, but you can't let them consume you. When you validate insecurities, they make you feel worse about yourself and reaffirms doubt's place in your relationship. You stop feeling worthy of any of the good parts of your relationship, which leads you to feel skeptical of why your partner would ever want to be with you without an exterior motive.

The insecurities you have that impact your relationship might not even be insecurities related to your partner. For example, maybe you're insecure about your body. You're not alone! A shocking seventy-one percent of Americans have reported, at times, feeling unsatisfied with their bodies. In contrast, a significant twenty-one percent reported that they *never* feel satisfied with their bodies. Women, young adults, and people with higher education degrees are even more self-critical of their bodies, showing how vulnerable people can be to this insecurity. This insecurity will carry over into your romantic life. It can impact sexual intimacy or even just how willing a person is to be emotionally vulnerable around their partner, because if you don't feel secure in yourself, it's hard to show yourself to other people who may reject you.

All the things you don't like about yourself will limit your ability to be who you are in a relationship, which will cause the other person to think that you're closed off or uninterested. Insecurity can breed insecurity. Going back to the body image example, for instance, surveys have shown that people correlate good sexual experiences with a good body image. Conversely, when people have bad sexual experiences, they may feel poorly about their bodies. Accordingly, the insecurities people have are all interrelated and will contribute to sexual and romantic problems. When you are insecure, you change the way you act. You avoid doing certain things and showing certain parts of yourself, but your partner may not recognize that you are insecure. Even in long-term relationships, partners may mistake your insecurities for you no longer loving them. Thus, by being insecure, your partner may also become insecure. They will start to doubt your relationship and withdraw from it so that they don't get hurt (just like you would). In the process, you both shut down and stop being able to communicate in the way you should. The moment you let insecurity control you are when you start to lose control of your relationship.

The mere fact that you fight with your partner isn't a sign; there is a genuine problem in your relationship. When handled appropriately, battling can enhance your relationship. If you never deal with, and never talk about your issues, you will never solve them. By taking care of problems constructively, you can obtain a better understanding of your companion and come up with an option that helps both of you. On the other hand, it is likewise feasible for problems to escalate and create hostility without fixing anything. How can you boost the odds of a successful resolution to the disputes in your relationship? Here are eight research-backed suggestions:

1. Be straight.

Occasionally, individuals do not merely come out and clearly state what is troubling them. Instead, they select more indirect ways of expressing their annoyance. One companion might condescendingly talk to the other and display their underlying hostility. Other times, partners may mope and frown without genuinely dealing with the issue. Companions may prevent discussing an issue by swiftly changing topics when the subject becomes incredibly elusive. Such indirect ways of expressing temper are not useful since they don't point the individual toward the target of the behavior. They understand that their companion is irritated, but the absence of directness leaves them without advice regarding what they can do to solve the issue.

2. Discuss exactly how you feel without blaming your partner.

Declarations that directly assault your companion's character can be especially destructive to a relationship. If a guy frustrated by his sweetheart's envy claims, "You're unreasonable!" he is inviting her to become protective. Also, this can close any new conversation. Generally, habits concentrate on a specific action your partner is taking part in, as opposed to being a character flaw.

Nonetheless, it must be noted that these direct negative techniques can be constructive—in some circumstances. The study revealed that for couples with reasonably small troubles, criticizing one's companion during a problem was related to lower relationship fulfillment over time and tended to make issues worse.

3. Never say never (or "always").

When you're dealing with a problem, you must stay clear of generalizing about your partner. Statements like, "You never help around the house" or "You're constantly staring at your mobile phone" are likely to make your partner defensive. As opposed to promoting a discussion regarding how your companion could be more useful or mindful, this method is most likely to lead your companion to start producing counterexamples of all the times they *were* valuable or alert. Again, you don't want to place your companion on the defensive.

4. Listen to your partner.

It is not very encouraging to feel like your partner is not taking note of you. When you disrupt your partner or think that you already understand what they believe, you're not giving them a chance to share themselves. Even if you are positive that you recognize where your partner is coming from or know what they're going to claim, you could still be wrong. Your partner will again feel like you're not listening.

You can reveal to your partner that you're listening by utilizing energetic attention-giving methods. When your partner talks, listen. Paraphrase what they say—that is, rephrase it in your own words. This can avoid misconceptions before they begin. You can also perception-check, by ensuring that you're translating your companion's reactions appropriately.

5. Do not automatically object to your partner's complaints.

When you're being criticized, it's difficult not to get defensive. Remember, defensiveness doesn't address troubles. Envision a couple arguing because the wife wants her husband to do more duties around the house. When she recommends that he does a quick clean-up after he gets ready to leave in the morning, he claims, "Yes, that would certainly help, but I do not have time in the morning. We usually do chores on the weekends, and I have other work to catch up on, etc.,

etc..." This "yes, but" habit suggests that her concepts and views are also not beneficial. Another destructive, protective behavior is "cross-complaining," when you reply to your partner's problem with problems of your very own. For instance, responding to "You do not tidy up enough around the house" with "You're a clean fanatic." It is necessary to hear your partner out and consider what your partner is saying.

6. Take various viewpoints.

In addition to listening to your companion, you need to take his or her viewpoint and attempt to understand where they come from. Those who can gain their companion's perspective are less likely to become angry during an argument.

Various other research studies have revealed that taking a more unbiased point of view can be valuable. Couples who took part in this 20-minute writing exercise three times a year kept steady degrees of happiness in their marriage, while couples who didn't do the exercise showed decreases in relationship satisfaction.

7. Do not show contempt for your partner.

Of all the adverse things you can do and claim throughout a problem, the worst might be ridicule. Gottman has found that this is the leading cause of separations. Contemptuous statements are those that belittle your partner. This can involve mockery as well as name-calling. It can additionally include nonverbal actions like rolling your eyes or smirking. Such habits are incredibly rude and indicate that you're in conflict with your partner.

Think about a partner that claims, "I want you to take me out more." The other responds, "Oh yes, one of the most important things is to be seen out, as well as overpay for small portions of food at some rip-off dining establishment. Could you be shallower?" Or one partner states they're too worn out to clean up, as well as the many other responses.

This sort of ridicule makes it challenging to participate in an actual discussion. Also, it is likely to evoke anger from your companion, as opposed to an honest effort to address the real problem.

8. Know when it's time for a time-out.

If you see yourself falling under adverse patterns and finding that either you or your companion are not complying with the tips over, take a time-out from your disagreement. Even a short break for a couple of deep breaths can be enough to calm hot tempers.

What the research study on conflict shows is that understanding both viewpoints, as well as controlling your rage, are vital to handling disputes. Broadcasting your complaints can be useful for your relationship. However, problems must be masterfully handled, or you risk making them even worse.

How to Strengthen Your Relationship

Intimate relationships reflect the best and worst of all of us. They can provoke or ease our struggles. They can feel like magic when they're perfect.

Even when they are exactly right, anxiety will steal the magic and loosen the bond between two individuals who belong together. All relationships call for trust, tenderness, flexibility, and vulnerability. The problem is that, often, anxiety will erode relationships almost as easily as they were formed.

Even if you're someone dealing with anxiety, there are plenty of other traits about you that will make it easy to fall in love with you. All relationships have struggles, and the difficulties can be very common and quite natural, particularly when anxiety is at play.

Anxiety can function in interesting ways, and it can have different impacts on different relationships. Not all the following will apply to each relationship.

Here are some ways to improve and secure your relationship from the effects of anxiety:

Top up the emotional capital

You are likely to be extremely sensitive to the needs of others and offer your relationship freely and abundantly. However, anxiety can also drain the resources out of the relationship almost as quickly as you spend them. That's okay—there is plenty of good that comes with loving you to make up for this—but it may mean that you've got to keep making sure those benefits are balanced. Flood your partner with love, appreciation, and affection. Provide lots of touching and talking with him or her whenever you can.

Let your partner see you as a source of support

People with anxiety often have too much energy—without it, it is difficult to cope with anxiety. Make sure that your partner knows it doesn't matter how big or small their challenges are, sometimes you can be the strong one too. The inclination may be for anxious people's spouses to throw off their fears, but that might mean they eliminate the ability to feel nurtured and protected by you, which would be a great loss for both of you. Nothing is more relieving than the support of the person you love.

Let your partner in on whatever you think

Anxious thoughts are supremely personal but let your partner in on them. It is a big part of intimacy. Often, you'll talk about what you need to do to feel safe, what feels bad to you, and what could go wrong. You'll also have a great capacity to think about other people— anxious people do—but make sure you unite in the feelings that control you. Holding stuff in and keeping it to yourself tends to increase the gap between you and your partner.

It's perfectly fine to ask for reassurance—just not too much

Anxiety has a way of creeping through it all. It can make you question the stuff that doesn't deserve to be questioned when it's left unchecked—such as your connection. Asking your partner for reassurance is okay and very natural.

Place Yourself Open

The fear may have various effects on relationships. It could stoke the need for constant reassurance in some people. It may cause them to hold back in others, lessening their susceptibility to a heart attack. Vulnerability is beautiful—being vulnerable to another—and it is the core of good, stable relationships. The problem with over-protecting yourself is that it may encourage the very rejection you're trying to avoid. Part of intimacy is bringing someone in deeper than the rest of the world is allowed to be. Intimacy is trusting the other person with your delicate, messy, untamed bits—the bits that are always amazing, often baffling, and fine with the person who loves you.

Be Aware That Anxiety Is Creeping into Your Relationship

Sometimes, nothing can cause anxiety—that's one of the terrible things about it—so it's going to look for a goal, an anchor to hold it still and make sense. When you're in an intimate relationship, the bulls' eye will sit there, pulling your fear into its gravitational pull. This can create suspicions, envy, distrust, and insecurity. Remind yourself that this doesn't mean there is anything to worry about just because you're feeling concerned. If you have to worry, then see it for what it is—fear and not reality. You're happy, you're nervous, and you're good. Let the truth hold you up.

When it comes to feelings, Let Your Partner in

Humans are dynamic creatures and having someone close to you is the lifeblood of love and your story—even if it's someone who has been with you for a while. Individuals change, stories change, and it's easy to lose contact with the person who sleeps next to you at night, even in the most intimate relationship. When it comes to your fear, let your partner in. Talk about your feelings, about how you are affected by anxiety, your job, friendships, family, and how grateful you are for their love and support.

Let the Partner Know What's Happening You

Is there a particular circumstance that appears to shed light on your anxiety? Massive crowds? Overcoming hardships? Loud music in your car? Is he late? Speak to your partner so that if you unwontedly find yourself in the situation, he or she can understand what is happening.

Negative Core Beliefs

Core beliefs are the beliefs we have about ourselves, others, and the world around us; they have been in place since childhood, evolving from past experiences. They stick with people their entire lives, as a mechanism that helps them predict new situations. Due to these beliefs, we know how to behave and respond in different situations.

These beliefs can be positive and negative. If you had positive experiences in the past, your beliefs would also be positive. For example, if you grew up with parents who loved each other and did not hide it, you will have a positive view of love. You will likely seek out a partner who fits into the picture of a perfect relationship, based on what your parents impressed on you.

However, if you grew up with negative experiences such as one of your parents abandoning your family, you will grow up with a negative belief in all relationships. You may have a core belief in abandonment, which makes you afraid of your partner leaving you, and your behavior reflects this fear in negative ways. This behavior, in turn, will continue to hurt your relationship until you can learn to deal with the problem. The beliefs you have will determine how you see yourself. It determines to what extent you believe yourself to be worthy, competent, powerful, safe, and loved. The negative thoughts you have about yourself, others, and the world are damaging to relationships and should be dealt with accordingly.

Since core beliefs have their roots in the early stages of human development, they are challenging to overcome, but not impossible. They are seen as absolute truths about oneself, others, and the world. When triggered, negative beliefs can cause strong emotions that make you feel shame, depression, loss, anger, and more. There are two methods of overcoming these beliefs. One is better management of the situations that trigger them, and the other is to manage the behavioral reactions that follow.

As mentioned, our beliefs come from our childhood, which often means we continue to think like children even in adulthood. Ignoring consequences, we favor instant gratification instead of looking at the long-term outcome. We also rely on stereotypes and prejudices developed during childhood. We often react based on our emotions, and we do not use objectivism and logic to observe our situation. We are aggressive, vengeful, and we don't listen to others. To learn how to behave and not trigger these negative beliefs, we must understand them by thoroughly understanding the positive and negative that applies to us.

Identifying your Beliefs

Core beliefs work on an unconscious level, and this makes them hard to identify. People are often unaware of them, as they hide deep in the subconscious mind, and they are believed to be part of the basic survival instinct and defense mechanisms. However, if you don't try to become aware of these beliefs and accept them, you will never be able to change your behavior. Thus, your relationships will continue to be influenced or even ruined by them.

There are many ways to identify which beliefs you possess. Cognitive-behavioral therapy can test your views, or you can explore them by following the downward arrow technique. This means that when a thought pops into your head, you will have to examine it and follow it back to where it originated. Here is an example:

Let's say you think you are lazy. Ask yourself what this means and what it tells you. You may discover that you procrastinate too much, and it is because you think you will fail anyway, so why even bother. Ask yourself again. What does this mean about you? You could come up with an answer such as "I am weak" or "I am not competent enough." Continue asking yourself, "What does this mean about me?" until you have no more answers. The last one you come up with is your core belief. In this case, it might be that you do not think you are good enough.

There are many negative core beliefs, but let's label the most common ones. They often come in the form of a thought that sounds like any of the following:

1. I am not good enough.
2. I am unlovable.
3. I am incompetent.
4. I am unsure.
5. I am always wrong.
6. I am defective.
7. I am powerless.
8. I am worthless.

You may notice that all these phrases start with "I am." They are negative core beliefs that you have about yourself. When you try to predict how others feel about you, or what they think about you, it is called having a supportive belief. For example:

1. Nobody loves me.
2. Nobody supports me.
3. Nobody thinks I can do it.
4. Everyone thinks I'm stupid.
5. Everyone believes I'm incompetent.

Supportive beliefs are not real core beliefs. They are simply there to reinforce the core beliefs. When your core beliefs tell you "I am unlovable" thoughts such as "nobody loves me" are there to support it.

Once you have identified your negative core beliefs, you can start working on overcoming them.

How Negative Beliefs Affect Your Relationships

Negative beliefs influence the way we start a new relationship, but they also change the way we maintain the existing ones.

The most common beliefs that influence romantic relationships include belief of abandonment, emotional deprivation, insecurity, and failure. We often think of them as follows:

1. My loved one will abandon me.

2. My loved one will hurt me.

3. My loved one doesn't love me back.

4. My loved one will not protect me.

5. My loved one will see how unlovable I am.

Core beliefs are triggered because you find yourself in situations that unconsciously remind you of past experiences. Negative core beliefs are easy to trigger because they are based on fear. The behavior that follows them is the one that will determine how your relationship will be affected. Such beliefs can make you irrational, dependent, clingy, and make you lash out in anger. All these behaviors may influence your relationship in a negative way, so they must be changed. Don't expect your partner to be responsible for the way you react in certain situations; you must work on happiness. You can't rely on your partner to unite the situation, to mind your feelings, and to be cautious not to trigger your unfavorable ideas. Your partner is human too, and he is dealing with his own set of negative thoughts, emotions, and beliefs.

Overcoming Negative Beliefs

We already mentioned that there are two ways of overcoming core beliefs. We will discuss how to do it and what results you should expect.

Managing your situation

Negative beliefs are triggered by specific situations, conversations, and people, and the goal is to keep them from influencing the choices you make in your relationship. They will be the determining factor of what type of personality a person you find attractive might possess. Based on your past experiences, you might find it easy to attach yourself to individual personalities that often trigger core beliefs. This is how your mind distorts reality and makes wrong attachment figures attractive. A person with abandonment beliefs was most likely attached to a figure who abandoned him during childhood. This person will find people who have a predisposition to leave him to be the most attractive ones and he will seek them as partners. It is essential to make a conscious decision not to attach yourself to people who trigger your core beliefs.

Here is a list of possible personalities that will trigger your own core beliefs:

1. Abandoner: This person is most likely already involved in a relationship with someone else. He or she is unpredictable, unable to commit, and doesn't have a set plan. They are not very supportive, and they are often unavailable exactly when you need them.

2. Abuser: This person will lie, manipulate, and cheat. They are untrustworthy and unsafe. They will abuse you emotionally and/or physically. They will harm you and make you feel like you deserve it, as if you are the one to blame for everything.

3. Depriver: This person will avoid forming an attachment to you. They will close themselves off emotionally and add little value for your life together. They will often be unable to give you the relationship you are longing for.

4. Judge: This is the type of personality that will always judge your achievements, thoughts, and emotions. He will find flaws in you and will expose them to others. He will disrespect you and believe that you are not good enough for him.

5. Critic: This person will compare you to themselves, and to others. They will criticize your every move, and they will make you feel incompetent.

Avoid these types of personalities and you will avoid the negative situations they will pull you into. It makes a difference if someone is triggering your core beliefs frequently or just occasionally. We all have various beliefs, and they will eventually be triggered unintentionally by others, so if it happens on a rare occasion, this person might still be worth your attention. With effort, both of you can find happiness in a fruitful relationship.

Managing Your Behavior

You must be perfectly aware of the negative core beliefs you possess so you can recognize them when triggered. Once triggered, there is no opportunity to avoid the situation. The only thing you can do is try to manage your reactions and behaviors properly. Try writing down what you were doing when your ideals were triggered, how you behaved, and what actions you took. For example, let's say you have a failure belief, meaning you are afraid of not being good enough. You find yourself in a situation where your partner is giving you constructive criticism. It can be something as simple as telling you how to improve your recipe for a special dessert. Your failure belief is triggered, and you start comparing yourself to others, maybe to his mother's cooking abilities. You might react by avoiding the discussion, or you might begin criticizing your partner in return. To change your behavior and outbursts, you must recognize your positive core values, and try your best to focus on them.

Core values are the principals we hold in high regard, and we do our best to live by them. They can be honesty, faith, commitment, loyalty, optimism, courage, and so on. Ask yourself what your values are and write them down. It would be best if you practice your core values as often as possible. Next time your negative beliefs are triggered, try to react with your values in mind. Instead of avoiding the discussion, be courageous, and confront it. Instead of criticizing others when you feel angry, remind yourself how highly you value peace and respond calmly and logically.

Practice this behavior every day. Put yourself in situations where your values can become known. Volunteer, help others, and offer support. The more practice you have when your core beliefs are stable, the better you will respond once they are not.

ANXIETY IN RELATIONSHIPS
THERESA WILLIAMS

CHAPTER 4

"Jealousy - Why it happens and dealing with it"

Chapter 4: Jealousy – Why It Happens and Dealing with It

One of the fundamental reasons for jealousy originates from a period in an individuals' life when emotional damage is done, which assaults their reality or, eventually, their feelings of internal securities. These instabilities will truly influence a woman's confidence, which will bring about feelings of low self-esteem and doubt, eliminating any sense of pride. These emotional injuries can be brought about by physical and mental abuse and traumas, or an over-prohibitive or dominated adolescence. If a child is sexually assaulted, his or her security is compromised through confiding in the offender. Quite often, the child grows up feeling guilty for what happened to them. This is also validated when she's an adult and still feels responsible.

When a child is mentally abused, they normally carry on the existence of long-suffering verbal abuse and degrading. It happens to grown-ups in their relationships as well. The over-prohibitive or dominating childhood starts in early adolescence and follows through into adulthood. These abuses transform into profound emotional wounds.

These wounds will make a person feel like they're in a prison of anxiety and instability. If they don't learn to classify them, execute them, and make them stronger, they'll never be free of them. Women often look for explanations to tackle the issue that they feel within themselves, continually achieving nothing.

They don't look for it in themselves. This is the mistake they make because they have several issues.

The human brain is made of two halves, which permits two different ways of reasoning—positive and negative. Unfortunately, as mentioned before, if an individual is abused or loses trust, it weakens their capacity to keep the balance between them. This is the point at which they'll be the victim of specific causes that will flare up the thing that prompts jealousy. You might be considering what these causes are. They are something like a recollection from the past. It can be a smell, an individual's laughter, an image, another woman, a feeling of dismissing, or a memory of your partner looking at you. There is a wide range of causes that can bring about negative feelings.

Negative relationship factors are distinct causes. It happens when a relationship severs because of trust issues brought about by unfaithfulness or sex addiction by one partner. This will follow them into each subsequent relationship if they can't get in control of their problems.

Jealousy isn't a problem that can be overlooked or pardoned. You should fear jealousy because the fear is what makes it a negative inclination. Have you, at any point, seen how quickly jealousy can change your relationship from cheerful to destructive? It's one of the worst feelings, and nobody would ever wish it on any person, even one they really dislike.

The negative emotions hiding behind jealousy will slowly reduce your love and change it to fraud, dishonesty, and hate. It will make you change from a happy person to someone overly suspicious and running away from the truth. Reality is jealousy's enemy. Jealousy always averts reality, even faster than it changes the positive thoughts to negative ones. It controls your mind and makes you think that a person you have a strong feeling for is not who they used to be. It makes you believe that they are a cheater, that they want someone else, are watching adult videos without your knowledge, will never tell you the truth, and misunderstand what you say to them, so you make a fool of yourself. They will laugh at you when you're begging for help. It'll make you feel bad until you feel like vomiting, and it'll make you uncertain. It makes your body feel different. You may break out into a sweat and cause your breathing to become rapid. If you've ever felt this way, I'm pretty sure that you know what I'm talking about.

This negative feeling will make you dread abandonment. This fear is a strong trigger to jealousy. It will capture and force you into suffocating or protecting what belongs to you until that individual can never again hurt because of your jealousy. It'll make you feel a profound desire to manipulate everything your partner thinks and does. Enabling jealousy to make your mind want to manipulate it is a sign of addiction. In this connection prison, your fragileness makes your relationship weak. You have to feel appended, and it'll consume the feeling of being secure and affect your self-esteem. A perfect illustration of a connection prison is fear of letting your partner out of your site, such as not letting him go to work because you're afraid that he'll meet someone and leave you for them.

Jealousy is like a medication. When you let it get to you, you can't control it anymore. You let it control you. You have now become a dependent thinker, subject to jealousy and power. Having desires like this is like an addict requiring drugs.

Jealousy is your addiction, and the adrenaline of being scared makes you feel like you're high. However, this isn't positive adrenaline; it's an unadulterated negative adrenaline surge. The main antidote to battle it is with some positive steps that can reinforce your capacity to reclaim your control and get free from that connection jail.

Jealousy won't rest until it makes a disappointing and intolerable condition that makes you the cause of the problems in your relationship. You've become the aggressor that you never wanted to be. You're jealous now! You're the reason for the unrest tossed into the world outside you. It's a world that can't, in any way, shape, or form, sympathize with your torment. You have nobody else but you in this jail. You're the only person able to feel the agony, the one whose desires are controlling the situation and avoiding the world. You will wind up being consumed by negative considerations every time you turn around.

Dealing with Jealousy

Ending jealousy is like altering every mental or behavioral response. It begins with consciousness. Awareness lets you see that the stories are not real in your head. If you are so straightforward, you no longer respond to the possibilities that your imagination might imagine. Jealousy and anger are emotional reactions that are not true in believing situations in your head. You should change what you think affects your imagination and remove these harmful emotional reactions. Even if the response is warranted, envy and rage are not good ways to cope with the situation to get what we want. Trying to change anxiety or resentment is like controlling a car skidding on ice. Your ability to deal with the situation will significantly improve if you can avoid the risk before you get there. This means addressing the beliefs that cause jealousy rather than trying to control your emotions.

Dissolving relationships permanently means changing the underlying beliefs of fear and unconscious expectations of what your partner is doing.

The steps to end jealous reactions permanently are:

1. Recover personal power so that you can control your emotions and stop reactive behavior.
2. Change your point of view so you can step back from your plot.
3. Be mindful that your convictions are not valid; this is distinct from scientifically "knowing" that the claims are not real.
4. Gain power over your focus so that you can actively select your mind's story and emotions.

Several factors establish the envy dynamic. As such, practical solutions will tackle multiple elements of values, experiences, feelings, and strength of personal will. You will leave the doors open to those negative emotions and behaviors if you lack one or more of these components.

You can step back from the story by practicing some simple exercises and refrain from being caught up in the emotional reaction. If you want to change your feelings and actions, you can do it. It only takes some willingness to acquire sufficient skills.

ANXIETY IN RELATIONSHIPS
THERESA WILLIAMS

CHAPTER 5

"Narcissistic abuse in relationship" and dealing with it"

Chapter 5: Narcissistic Abuse in Relationships

As much as you might have heard or read about narcissists, you are not necessarily wrong to build a relationship with one. You also need to know that you are not deliberately setting yourself on the path of self-destruction. Narcissists are quite romantic and can be charming. They are great lovers and can be friends. The truth is that they can be sensitive to how you feel and adjust to your needs.

However, narcissists can be very manipulative, and they are complicated people. Therefore, being in any sort of relationship, whether romantic or not, spiritual or professional, you need to know that it can be confusing, and you need to be prepared for the situation. Narcissists are complicated and sometimes hard to understand. You will find them very helpful and dependable to the point they will seem to care about you. The truth is their devotion and kindness are mostly to benefit themselves and further put them in control of things.

Forming a relationship with a narcissist is not uncommon. Many people are in a narcissistic relationship without even realizing it until they are too far into it. The victim often doesn't feel like leaving because his or her life is centered on the narcissist. It is difficult to let go of such a relationship. It could be because they are married and have kids. Also, dealing with an ex who is a narcissist can be quite difficult.

Narcissists are potentially harmful in many ways. How do you simply make the relationship work? How is it possible to build a healthy relationship with a narcissist? It is, indeed, possible, and maybe rewarding to have a relationship with someone who is a narcissist. Still, that relationship could be psychologically and emotionally draining. A narcissist usually lacks what it takes to build a strong relationship. They do not show consistent kindness, compassion, selflessness, reciprocity, compromise, and empathy. They drain the energy and spirit from their supposed partners, turning them into figurative punching bags.

What to Expect in a Relationship with a Narcissist?

Being in a relationship or having any connection with a narcissist has many challenges. Still, when you are aware of what to expect, you should know how to handle the relationship better so you can build a healthy one.

You Will Need to Make Some Sacrifices

To have a good life or relationship with a narcissist, you need to make many sacrifices to keep the relationship going. You will sacrifice a part of you, especially your beliefs and what you stand for. One of the expected constants is that you will be lied to over and over yet must accept it.

Narcissists are crafty and very manipulative. They are good at changing the narrative and altering reality into the version that suits them. In the end, they get you to agree to something that you didn't do. To keep narcissists happy, you will need to learn how to accept their version of reality as the truth of what has happened even when it is not. That way, you will always escape their fury and not be on the receiving end of their anger.

Part of the sacrifice is that you might never be praised for achieving something or rewarded for behaving well. At every opportunity, a narcissist will try to undermine your efforts. They are manipulative to the point where they call all the shots yet in a very shrewd way that makes it seem as though you are in control. They will let you make some decisions but then do something different and you have to appreciate them for doing that.

Building healthy relationships with narcissists mean you have to play a secondary role. You need to make sacrifices that will drain you in many ways.

To a Narcissist, No One Is to Be Trusted

Narcissists don't trust anybody except themselves. Even when you do everything right and have never given them any reason for not trusting you, they still will not respect you enough to allow you to lead your life without interference and surveillance. They may go to the extent of spying and stalking you.

Narcissists have a habit of tracking their partners. In a romantic relationship, narcissists are likely to install trackers without the knowledge of their partners. It could be on their phone or computer, and they feel no remorse about it. In fact, they are rather proud of their actions.

Regrettably, most narcissists abuse drugs and alcohol to the extreme. Their partners will have to endure the abuse, adapt to their lifestyle, and live with the perpetual fear and expectation that they may take things too far with the drugs or alcohol and act unpredictably.

Most narcissists develop bad habits and, because of this, will become so irresponsible that they begin missing appointments, meetings, and work. Therefore, it puts their partners in situations where they have to clean up the mess they create and make up excuses to absolve them. The partners have been conditioned to believe that they are a team and that it's them against the whole world.

Narcissists will never put their trust in anyone; therefore, they use words that will keep their victims spellbound like "You are my world" and "Without you, I'm nothing." That way, their victims are comforted with a false sense of security. Meanwhile, they are just keeping their partners from everyone and everything, pitching them against the world and using them.

Narcissists will say things and take actions that are convincing enough to make you believe in them, trust them, and risk it all for them. You should be prepared to not be trusted when in a relationship with a narcissist.

Although it is not clear if narcissists do things intending to hurt their partners to the level they do, they give the excuse of having a bad childhood. You must understand and forgive them for all their shortcomings and behaviors. They will explode, and you will face their rage if you don't forgive them for everything they have done, including the times when they abused you.

You Will Be Drained and Tapped Out

Narcissists don't like taking the blame for anything. They look for someone else to take the blame, and you who have a relationship with one will likely be the person to fill that role. Therefore, to make your relationship work, you will have to come to terms with the fact that you are going to be the scapegoat at every opportunity and probably be demeaned. If you don't want to take the blame for them, the narcissistic traits will kick in, and they will accuse you of being crazy and inconsiderate. Mostly, all your feelings will be used against you to make you feel bad.

To make such a relationship work, you should be ready to put your self-interest behind you and be prepared to be harassed because everything that goes wrong is your fault. You will need to lose yourself. The things you love, the things you like, the fun things you do, your music choice, books, and movies will all be termed bad or uncool. To them, you have terrible taste. They will gradually mold you into somebody you are not.

To keep a narcissist happy, you might need to lose your friends, family, and even your job. You might have to stop pursuing your career and interests. You will have to live for them to be happy. Your life will revolve around them to keep the relationship going and keep them happy. You will stay home all-day doing chores. Still, all that won't get you any accolades. They will then call you a boring person. Some narcissists would rather have you keep your job so that you can help keep their lifestyle financed, milking you while you slave for their happiness.

By now, you have most likely determined that you are in a one-way relationship with a very self-centered person. You have, in all probability, learned a good deal about your relationship. Most likely, you are considering making some changes. Are you willing to do things differently in your relationship with your loved one? This chapter will help you explore whether you are ready to make some important changes and will then give you some new strategies for managing the narcissist in your life.

Deciding If You Are Ready

Change almost always involves overcoming some of your anxieties and taking risks involving your personal growth. You will need to overcome your anxieties about change before you can begin to do things differently. You may ask yourself, "Are changes possible?" and "Should I make them?" Now is the time to make some important choices. You will need to answer some tough questions.

Can You Forgive and Move forward?

Forgiveness is the starting point. Most likely, your one-way relationship has hurt you in many ways, and you have needed to forgive your partner, friend, or relative in the past, but you will need to do it again. You cannot harbor resentment and maintain a good relationship. Sooner or later, you will have to forgive the narcissist, and the sooner, the better. Fortunately, we are billionaires in forgiveness; we have an endless supply. Remember, you do not have to feel forgiving to forgive; it is an act of will, a decision you make, not a feeling. Also, forgiving does not mean foolishly if the narcissist will not do more hurtful things in the future; he probably will, and you should be on the alert so as not to be taken advantage of. It may be helpful to remember that forgiveness is also for you. By letting go, you can begin to heal too.

Are You Willing to Work on Just Yourself?

Another prerequisite for change is that you need to accept that you can only change yourself. Can you resist the temptation of trying to change the narcissist? It's easy to fall back into old patterns, especially when success is not immediate. You may find yourself asking, "Why do I have to change when he is the problem? Shouldn't it be fifty-fifty?" Quite frankly, we have never known a relationship to be fifty-fifty. Besides, making changes is empowering because you are in control. Waiting around for others to change just makes you feel weak and angry. You may think it's unfair that you will have to do all the work now since you're the only one who has worked for this relationship all along—after all, it's one-way! But most likely, you have worked in the wrong areas, especially if you have been trying to change the narcissist.

Is Your Loved One Capable of Loving You the Way You Need to Be Loved?

To put it bluntly, would you bet on a horse that has never won a race? If the narcissist in your life has never had a successful reciprocal relationship, you are making this bet. Oh, sure, the narcissist will claim to love you, but there are many types of love. At two years old, a baby loves his mother, but that is not the type of love you look for in a romantic partner or a friend. The narcissist's level of love is immature, but it is all that he knows. Can he grow in his level of maturity in loving? That is a tough one to call. Past success is a good predictor: Have you seen any maturation since you have known him? If so, there is hope.

Are You Ready to Get the Help You Need?

You should seriously consider getting professional help in your one-way relationship. We recommend finding an expert who has a history of working with narcissistic clients. Narcissists can be quite challenging for therapists, especially those who are not trained to work with them, so it's important to put some effort into finding someone with the right experience. A good resource might be a local university with a graduate program in clinical psychology, or you can try the Institute for Advanced Studies in Personality and Psychopathology in Port Jervis, New York, or the Personality Disorders Institute at Cornell University. Both institutes train clinicians to treat narcissistic people and may be able to recommend an expert in your area. (See resources for more information.) When contacting a professional, you will want to make an appointment for yourself; if the narcissist agrees to come, all the better. True friends and trusted family members can also be a good source of emotional support and encouragement, and you'll need them if you decide to make changes. There is also a good deal of reading material on narcissism, including information on the Internet. You will want to read all you can and become an expert. At the very least, you will know more about the topic than the narcissist in your life.

Eliminate negative thinking in relationships

Your mind is like a garden, and we are the master gardener enthusiasts. Through care and persistence, we can produce an agricultural masterpiece, but through neglect, our yard will be a mass of weeds— downsides, instabilities, and failures. Understanding this, it becomes our duty to remove negative thinking. There are four exceptional techniques for removing the downsides from your mind. Each method is unique and independent from the others. Several of these strategies will undoubtedly seem inconsistent. However, each will be very effective in dealing with negative thinking.

1. Cut it off.

With this method, the moment you identify that you are assuming a negative idea, you end it. You do not stay with it, you do not analyze it, you do not shield against it on your own. The moment you realize that you are thinking about an unfavorable idea, just make the right choice in your mind.

2. Tag it.

As quickly as you acknowledge that you are considering a negative thought, rather than cutting it off, as with the first technique, tag it. Write it down in bold letters and read it at least three times before you continue. You want it to be imprinted into your mind. **Obstacles only have power over you if you respond to them.**

Go back and read it again. Continue to read this statement until you realize that reacting to problems is what provides power to it. The minute you begin worrying, start responding to the negative, and start taking the blame, it has taken over you. When you acknowledge that the negativity only has power over you when you respond to it, then you made a choice not to react. Tag it. Remember that it is only a negative idea and then move on to another thing. Don't get trapped into thinking about it. Disregard it. Once again, they only have power over you if you react to them.

3. Overemphasize the assumed into all ridiculousness.

The overestimation technique is a fantastic method; however, you must exaggerate it right into ridiculousness. The keyword is ridiculousness. Imagine that you're a salesperson out making your sales calls when the thought comes to you, "Ah, what's the use? I'm not going to make any more sales today." Afterward, you decide on your own, "Wait a second… that's an unfavorable thought." With the exaggeration method, what you might say next is, "That's right, I'm not likely to make another sale today."

I wouldn't be shocked if, as quickly as I open the door; people are ready to throw buckets of water at me. After that, they're most likely to launch pit bull terriers as well as German guards. I'm going to be attacked as well as I'm going to be wet. Then this great big mechanical boxing glove will undoubtedly appear, and it's most likely to smash me in the face.

Wouldn't it be wonderful if, when we have negative thoughts, they include warning signs reading, "It's only an adverse thought; you do not need to believe it if you don't want to." Yet, problems do not come like that. They come camouflaged as genuine issues, or silently, when we're not paying attention. If we're not knowledgeable about the fact that our mind is a fantastic impostor, forever invoking unpleasant thoughts, we'll buy into every devastating idea that strikes us. However, with these methods, we have ways of taking care of the negative issues. That's why they are so useful.

4. Combat the negative with the exact opposite.

Whenever the undesirable is clinging to you, you can neutralize it by believing the exact opposite. When the negative thinking concerns you, "I'm not going to make another sale today," you offset it with, "I'm most likely to make several more sales today." When the adverse idea takes control of you, "I'm never going to get ahead monetarily," you counteract it with the exact reverse, "I'm most likely to be enormously successful monetarily." When the thought comes to you, "I'm never going to have a meaningful relationship," you neutralize it with the opposite, "I'm going to have a fabulous relationship." You see, the mind can think just one thought at a time so make it positive.

It might seem to you that you're assuming many thoughts at once, yet what is taking place is you're thinking one idea after another, after another, and more. At any given minute, you're only thinking one idea. So, if you secure the difficult thoughts and do the exact opposite, you are taking power away from that unfavorable thought. Don't feed the beast. Frequently, this is contrary to what most people do. Most individuals, when there is something that they don't intend to have happen to them, they think about it, and they focus on it. Eventually, they can materialize it.

Try To Rebuild a New Life

When you're forced to recognize that you have lost the person you assumed was "the one," it resembles starting from scratch. Your life, as you once understood it, disappears and you find yourself standing there alone, trying to find out what's next. Your self-confidence is shot. The future you had planned on is now gone and it's hard to not feel confused or too terrified. In addition, there is the pain of such a loss. However, people are resilient; we can get better from this kind of dissatisfaction. We have the capability to turn things around, make favorable adjustments for our future, and rebuild everything that has been shed. Of course, you're doing all that restoring on your own, but after losing "the one," it's better to be alone for a while anyway. Believe me on this one!

Talk It Out

I honestly believe that everyone who's rid themselves of a person they thought they'd invest their lives with must enter treatment. Speaking with an expert can seriously help you to grow. If you're brand new to therapy, know that it's experimentation. You may not love the first couple of therapists you meet, so do not settle. You're about to have a very intimate relationship with this person as you "spill the beans" concerning your entire life to them, so you need to find a person who makes you feel comfortable.

If professional treatment isn't for you, talk with another person in your life who is encouraging, whether it is a pal, coworker, family member, etc.

Modification of Your Environment

If you intend to change your life, you will also need to change the things you have around you. Moving halfway around the world sounds wonderful. Theoretically, it's not the most effective move to make. Instead, make changes to the environment where you already live. For example, I painted my walls, tossed out all my bedding in exchange for new much more vivid ones, and repositioned my furniture. When you're reconstructing your life, you need to concentrate on you, what you desire, and what changes make sense in this new phase.

Look for What Interests You

To restructure, you need to put yourself out there. You need to grow, meet new people, sign up for courses, as well as go out to events— generally anything that ignites your interests. You might enroll in some courses that you think are intriguing before finding something that's the right fit. Regardless, you're not just creating the necessary interruption that we all require after losing "the one," but you're concentrating on what benefits this brand-new you.

Have Some Flings

Although, it will absolutely take some time to return to dating once again, when you are preparing, have a few flings. Don't try to delve into something major, but instead, date several people and enjoy some variety. Date people that aren't your type. Have casual sex with a person you would have never considered having casual sex with before you got rid of "the one." You should think about this part of your life as a transitional period, and a necessary one, before you agree to fully open your heart once more.

Create a Happiness Routine

You can't just dream all day. You need to create a regimen that brings you bliss, to produce energy and knowledge to trust on your own how to load your cup initially.

Start by making a list of points you delight in doing to take care of your mind and soul. It could be having tea in the morning, taking a walk, or listening to an inspirational podcast. Whatever it is, make a checklist and pick three points you can do every day that will sustain your soul. This goes to developing a routine of caring and will be excellent for you.

CHAPTER 6

"The importance of communicating with your partner"

Chapter 6: The Importance of Communicating With Your Partner

Communication is the key to any successful relationship. If you fail to communicate effectively, it can lead to misunderstandings, hurt feelings, and many other issues. Mindful communication is all about being more conscious about the way you interact with the other person daily. It is about being present when the other person is communicating with you. This is especially important in a relationship. Your partner needs you to be present and they want to see that you can listen to and understand their thoughts and feelings. However, real communication has become increasingly difficult these days.

People are more comfortable texting each other or using social media than having actual face-to-face conversations. No matter where you look, people are looking down at their phones instead of facing the person sitting right next to them. It doesn't matter if it's on a date or if the person is sitting right next to you at home. Think about it. How often do you really communicate with your partner?

Take some time to notice if you do any of the following things:

- Forming responses before your partner finishes their sentence
- Thinking of something else, even when your partner is talking to you
- Feeling impatient during a conversation
- Cutting your partner short when they speak

- Thinking about your own experience when it relates to something that happened to your partner
- Feeling bored when you have to discuss something or have a real conversation

These are some of the common communication patterns that have developed between people today. All of it harms your life and your relationship with your partner. This is where mindful communication comes to the rescue. Whether you want to improve your relationship with your partner or work on your social skills in general, mindfulness adds the necessary dimension to successful communication.

Committing to mindful communication with your partner means you will be committing to the following:

- Listening to your partner without being distracted
- Holding a conversation without being too emotional
- Being non-judgmental when you talk, argue, or fight with your partner
- Accepting your partner's perspective even if it is different from yours
- Validating yourself and your partner

All of these are important and will benefit your relationship in so many ways.

Relationship Communication

As you know, communication is particularly important when it comes to romantic relationships. Being able to discuss all issues freely, make plans, and set goals for the future are vital for a successful relationship. Otherwise, how could two partners handle their responsibilities, challenges, and expectations?

However, what happens if one of you is suffering from anxiety? Of course, it depends on how severe the anxiety is. Even so, no matter its level of development, the personal connection will be in some way affected.

You or your partner might encounter difficulties reacting in a healthy way when either of you expresses an opinion or an emotion. For instance, it is common to misread someone's intent or misinterpret the meaning of individual conversations. Anxiety works in many ways as a filter. When it clouds your vision, you might act in a way that will eventually damage your relationship. Any joke, comment, or harmless critique can lead to an overreaction that will strain any couple, even more than the anxiety itself.

If you find yourself in such a situation, you should take a break and figure out what warranted such a negative reaction or outburst. Your partner may be suffering from a form of anxiety, and they are overwhelmed by the strain. On the other hand, if you are the one with this problem, you need to acknowledge what's wrong and express it. If you don't, your partner will think you're being cruel or aggressive for no reason, or that they are the problem.

Relationship Communication Anxiety

Anxiety has a severe emotional effect on people. The partner is always affected in some way because of seeing his or her significant other suffering and going through a life-crippling experience. In many cases, the one suffering from anxiety will suppress emotions or feelings. Emotions carry a great deal of power, and some people find it too challenging to face them. Those who are afraid to express themselves emotionally have likely lived in a household where this behavior was discouraged.

The act of suppressing emotions is a sign that the person is trying to hold onto a semblance of control. If you find yourself behaving this way, it might be because you fear losing that control and allowing the locked-up feelings to overwhelm you. Naturally, the biggest issue here is when it comes to negative emotions, as they have such a substantial impact on a person's life. You might think that if you let it all out, you will change your partner's feelings and whatever good opinions and thoughts he or she has about you will be gone, cause damage to the relationship. However, while you may think of this as a solution, it leads to even more problems. Acting this way will increase the amount of anxiety you experience. You will find less peace of mind, until one day when it will all come out in a wild burst. It's difficult to suppress those feelings forever, and when they come to the surface, they will cloud all judgment.

Communication anxiety can also manifest itself without involving any emotional suppression. For instance, let's say your partner unloads only his most powerful feelings and emotions regularly. Some people cannot hold back on certain beliefs, so they lash out. As a result, both of you end up feeling overwhelmed and confused, leading to another problem. Experiencing these outbursts often enough, you can start feeling that it's your job to find a solution to your partner's issues. It's not enough to notice the anxiety and the strain it's putting on your relationship. You begin to get the feeling you are the sole savior of the relationship. Unfortunately, this usually makes things worse, as your partner could start developing resentment towards you for their behavior.

Another communication problem is when you consider expressing yourself as a risky affair. Maybe you are wondering what will happen if you reveal what you honestly think. It is enough to trigger your anxiety because you are afraid of the uncertainty of the outcome. Frequently, this symptom stems from not having confidence in yourself, and you are worried about an adverse reaction from your partner. In this case, you might be taking a great deal of time to rehearse what you will say and complicate things further by imagining all the possible scenarios.

Lessons from Mindful Communication

Mindful communication will help you learn some invaluable lessons. Here are a few:

You will learn to listen to your partner.

Being a good listener is very important, and it is something that your partner needs from you. Don't respond without listening to them and let them complete their sentences. Look them in the eyes when they talk and show them that you are paying attention. Please pay attention to their words and their body language. Try to understand what they are trying to convey to you. Listening well can help you know and understand your partner much better. It will also show your partner that you care. Make them more comfortable around you. They will feel valued and will know that they can depend on you.

You will learn to be non-judgmental.

You will learn how to be non-judgmental and provide a safe space for your partner to communicate with you. People are often afraid of conveying their true feelings or opinions when they think the other person will judge them. If you have a judgmental attitude, your partner will refrain from speaking honestly to you, as well. This means they don't feel comfortable with you and might look for this level of understanding from someone else. Be encouraging to your partner and let them know you respect their opinion, regardless of how different your own is.

You will view problems more objectively.

People often react in the wrong way when their personal opinions or emotions cloud their judgment. Being objective is crucial if you want to truly resolve issues. If not, you will not be able to have a productive or honest conversation. This is important to foster growth and solve problems in your relationship. It would help if you kept your partner's perspective in mind before you reply to them. The more time you take to consider their view, the better you will be able to solve the problem in an even-tempered way.

You will be able to control your life better.

Mindful communication, and mindfulness in general, can help you find more clarity in life. It will help you to avoid small problems that are often caused by bad communication. You will learn how to control your emotions and take control of how you handle different situations.

You can see that mindfulness in communication can help you truly connect with your partner.

Mindfulness will help you to understand your partner and maybe even learn from them. Your relationship will be strengthened, and you will be able to make better choices for your overall benefit. Don't doubt the value of good communication skills.

You will notice how you can apply mindfulness in various situations and in different ways when you communicate with your partner.

This will help you improve yourself as a person and increase personal growth. You will learn how to stabilize your relationship and take it in a positive direction, as well. Mindful communication can teach you how to get control over your thoughts, feelings, and actions in a positive way. Once you have this control, you can exercise it for your benefit. You will soon understand how some couples make it through thick and thin with the help of better communication.

Learning How to Listen to Your Partner.

Good conversation is not just about *what* you're doing, but *when* you're doing it. We all know a conversation consists of two people who talk in exchange, sharing knowledge for mutual benefit and (hopefully) enjoyment.

Unfortunately, in the hope of knowing them, too many of us are not listening to our discussion partner. We continue to listen only so that we know when we can take our place in the spotlight next time without being too rude!

This means that two people may have what seems to be a conversation, but in fact, it is a simple game of "When do I get to talk next?" This kind of "conversation" is a total waste of time because no one gets the chance to know anything new and there is no real relationship.

Many of us are bad listeners, but we fail to recall what other people tell us. Speaker and communications specialist Julian Treasure states that, while we spend about 60 percent of our overall speaking time listening to other people, we don't pay attention.

On average, we retain just 25 percent of what we hear. He claims that over the years, we have slowly lost our ability to listen at high quality.

Why? In short, technology has made us lazy.

Since we've become accustomed to using copies of materials, books, images, and so on, we subconsciously assume that it doesn't matter if we're listening the first time, because we can play it back or read it again later.

Of course, the trouble is that you can't just fill in the blanks for a conversation Google had later. At this moment, you need to be listening and paying attention.

How to Practice Directing Your Attention

Fortunately, you can retrain your brain to tune in, pay attention to every sound in your world, close your eyes, and imagine how many different sound "channels" or "streams" you can hear at any given moment.

Give them labels, "talking men," "window rain," and so on. This strengthens the willingness to stay focused on what someone else says. Practice this exercise every day for several minutes and you will soon find a change in your ability to concentrate.

What Kind of Listening Do You Need to Do?

Were you aware that there are many ways we can listen to each other? These methods are called role listening. We may participate in critical versus empathic listening, reductive versus expansive listening, and active versus passive listening.

Many of us have heard about active and passive listening—and it has been said that active listening is usually what we should be doing—but listening can be a little more complicated than that. For example, you could adopt a critical, reductive, and an active role in any given conversation.

When you listen from a strategic position, you are evaluating the truth behind a case. For instance, if someone tells you about the new phone they've just purchased and how their features make it better than all the other models on the market, you might be able to judge their points while they're talking.

You may wonder why the phone does not have the biggest screen size, the fastest processor, etc. In this scenario, it scans every piece of knowledge, and you draw your conclusions.

By contrast, empathic listening is the art of honoring feelings over bare reality. If you have an empathetic approach to listening, the main goal is to help others express their feelings, simply by being present and paying attention.

By focusing on the emotions of others, you gain a better understanding of their thoughts and behaviors. It will come up in your facial expression, body language, and tone of voice. You can also experience a sense of comfort when you're listening style is a good fit for the topic of discussion and the other person's needs.

The disparity between reductive listening and expansive listening must also be acknowledged. You will engage in a reductive listening approach by listening to others to get to the most important points as soon as possible.

The listening posture is useful in high-pressure situations when faced with direct facts. For example, a surgical nurse who listens to the lead physician's instructions is participating in reductive listening. We need to home in on the facts as quickly as possible and then act upon it.

It is not necessary to minimize listening if a speaker does not know what he thinks, what he needs to say, or even how he feels. For this situation, you have to take another approach. You should sit calmly with the speaker as they work through their thoughts and feelings, rather than waiting for them to get straight to the point like you would when you are practicing reductive listening.

Expansive listening is like empathic listening in the sense that both positions value the speaker's feelings. Still, the former is more focused on finding insight than on providing an emotional outlet for others.

The most famous is active versus passive listening. In brief, active listening refers to the process of deliberately trying to hear what the other person is saying and to respond encouragingly, perhaps by summing up and asking questions.

In contrast, passive listening takes no effort. When you adopt a passive stance, you can take some of the information in, even if you don't hear it or completely understand it, you're not too bothered. Popular wisdom holds that active listening is often the preferred option. That is not a bad rule to live by. Nobody was ever insulted, after all, because everyone listened so well! Yet, occasionally, passive listening is all it takes.

Bad communicators believe that "listening" is merely the act of waiting for their turn to speak, all the while writing their answers mentally. That is a grave error. Listening is so much more than that—it's a way to allow someone else to express their thoughts and opinions, create emotional intimacy, and display empathy.

Listening is not just about allowing people to vocalize what's on their mind, although that is important. Listening also reflects the first step towards personal progress.

Psychotherapist Carl Rogers, one of the 20th century's most influential psychologists, noted that when someone allows us to think about what happened to us and how we feel about it, we begin to understand the best way to improve our emotions and behaviors.

Although it may be helpful to take advice from someone else, if we sort out ourselves through our issues, we are more likely to improve. One of the most important ways of doing this is to communicate openly to an informed audience.

Keep your tongue and give them the space they need if your conversation partner rambles, or if their words do not seem to make sense. Before implementing a strategy, they may want to speak to some other people first, or they might need to analyze the problem in their own time. You don't want to get angry! Extend to others the kindness you expect in exchange.

Top tips that will make you an outstanding listener

1. To encourage them to keep talking, use non-intrusive verbal and non-verbal gestures. Nodding and saying, "Uh-huh" and "I see" are brief, unobtrusive gestures that facilitate more disclosure. Silence is all right, too—occasionally, someone needs a couple of minutes to collect their thoughts before continuing the discussion. Give them some space.

2. Let them continue until they run out of steam. Once I learned to listen properly, I was shocked to discover that a lot of people want someone to slow down and hear what they have to say. This is particularly true if they feel frustrated, upset, or need to work through an issue.

One of the most important, simple—and challenging—listening skills of all is staying quiet and letting the other person hold the air. If you are dealing with an angry or frustrated person, they will not be able to think clearly, until they have offloaded everything on their mind.

3. Do not play the role of armchair psychologist. Everybody is a psychologist to some degree. We all want to come up with our hypotheses as to why so-and-so is so mad all the time, etc.

Do not worry about their motives, or why they act in a particular way, when sharing sensitive details with you. You're going to come off as a bit nosy at best. At worst, your partner in the conversation will feel patronized and furious.

4. Do not disturb unsolicited advice. Even though you may have been in the same position or faced the same issues as someone else, do not give them your suggestions and solutions until you have asked them if you could do so. There are very few things more irritating than unwelcome feedback or advice.

Try to resist the temptation to remind them that you know exactly what they are going through. Two people may have similar experiences, but their styles of personality, culture, and past life events ensure they won't feel the exact same emotions.

When your conversation partner asks for your feedback, go ahead, but take a look at their response. If they seem open to your suggestions, go ahead. If, however, they begin to frown, cross their arms, or offer some sign that your advice is not helpful or welcoming, then pause and ask if they want you to proceed.

Realize that they have no duty to obey your advice. Set aside your ego. Once you've invested in them, it's up to the other person to make their next strategic step. Also, they will not be sharing the whole story, so they may need to take into account other facts, so consider all the factors when drawing up an action plan.

5. Re-phrase the words of someone else, but don't parrot them again. You might have learned that repeating back the words of others indicates to them that you listened. That's correct, to a point. There is a fine line between expressing awareness and quoting others verbatim.

To demonstrate the definition, I shall use an illustration. Suppose your friend said, "I've been feeling very lonely lately. It seems my family doesn't know what I'm doing or whether I'm even content with that." Here are two possible responses. What do you think would help your friend feel noticed, and what would make them feel annoyed?

"So, you feel like they're not paying much attention to you right now?" or "You've been feeling sad lately, so it doesn't matter what you're doing with your family?" The second answer shows that you've heard the real words, but it also sounds strange! Your friend might wonder if, instead of a normal human being, she was talking to a parrot. I prefer the first response since, in addition to the words themselves, it reflects an absorption of the meaning behind the words.

CHAPTER 7

"Relationship mistakes with anxiety"

Chapter 7: Relationship Mistakes With Anxiety

When we see the world through an anxiety-stricken lens, it can be depressing trying to figure out what is worth worrying about and what is not. This can lead to feelings of confusion, shutting down your claims, or connecting with your partner as passive aggressive. Although it is not your fault, it is always helpful to remember how anxiety can affect the way you see things so that you can begin to move in a healthier direction.

If it feels like anxiety is holding you back, you might even choose to treat it—for your sake and your partner's sake. "Seeing a psychologist is one of the best things you can do when you have anxiety in your relationship," says Katie Ziskind, marriage, and family therapist.

1. Not Being Present with Your Partner (Being Absent)

One of the worst side effects of anxiety is being "checked out" or not fully present in your everyday life. While this sucks on its own, it can hurt your relationship as well.

Nevertheless, it is an issue that can be overcome. You can receive assistance from a loved one or a therapist who will show you how to cope with your fear and, therefore, feel more grounded.

2. Having Trust Problems

Because anxiety will make you feel like your life is spinning out of control, it is only because you won't necessarily feel safe and this can lead to confidence problems in your relationship.

Rosalind Sedacca, a dating and relationship coach, tells Bustle: "An anxious partner can be more jealous (or) nervous than others, wanting to know who (their partners) are calling, texting, and (or) meeting throughout the day. It can cause them to telephone or email (their partner) questioning (their) behavior too often and violating (their) privacy." Although it stems from anxiety, this behavior can still affect the relationship and cause your partner to imagine things. This is one more reason to seek ways of controlling anxieties and emotions so that they are not overwhelming.

3. Appearing as Controlling

"People who are anxious try to 'control' their lives and frequently cope with this," Sedacca says. It can start leaking into your relationship, which makes you feel controlling or manipulative towards your partner. While this is not your goal, and we must learn safer ways to cope, both of you can have a difficult time dealing with it—especially if you have to go to treatment.

4. Overthinking Every Single Thing

Do you want to overthink everything? This is a huge sign of anxiety, and it can affect your trust in opening to others—including your partner.

"The 'impacts' of what you say can affect you," Dr. DePompo says. But, if there is a person on the planet with whom you should be honest, it is your partner.

While some people can get used to it and some try to have big faith, try to stop "editing," says Dr. DePompo. It may be daunting at first, but you're certainly worth it with a supportive partner.

5. Taking Things Personal

Another side effect of anxiety is that it becomes all too easy to jump to conclusions, make the worst of a situation, and therefore take things personally.

It's crucial not to let your partner get out of control. "When [they are] distant, for example, a person with anxiety could take it personally instead of trying to have a conversation and figure out what could happen," Dr. Helen Odessky, author of *Stop Anxiety from Stopping You*, tells Bustle, a clinical psychologist. "Examples include stress at work, physical illness, and depression." It may be effective and train the brain—perhaps by using a therapist—to first consider these external causes before jumping to conclusions and picking fights with your partner.

6. Getting "Stuck" in Old Habits

Relationships must be established and improved to stay healthy. For someone with anxiety, this can be incredibly difficult.

"People with fear stop trying new things, taking chances, and letting go," says Dr. DePompo. "This can keep the stuff standing overnight—

you need a spark to kindle a fire. If you are, try things irrespective of how confident you like them—let them know about the experience and shake it about the perfectionism of 'the best' choices."

7. Always Expecting Your Partner to Cure Your Anxiety

While your partner should be aware of your anxiety and be as supportive as possible, it will not help to put pressure on them to cure it for you. "If we expect them to assuage every fear or constantly provide reassurance, we are putting them in a position that they are not meant to occupy namely, taking responsibility for our anxiety," says Julie Williamson, LPC, NCC, RPT, a licensed professional counselor. "Not only is this not fair to your partner, but it's also not fair to you because it's impossible for your partner to cure your anxiety."

8. Replying Passive-Aggressively

"As anxiety may lead to feelings of irritability, you may be lashing out or responding to your partner in passive-aggressive ways," says Williamson. You might also find that you can't talk to your partner without the conversation going downhill quickly.

9. Venting to an Unhealthy Extent

If you aren't coping with your anxiety in a healthy way, don't be surprised when you make the mistake of relieving venting with your partner all the time. While it's okay to let a bit of steam off and share some tense parts of your day, it can become a burden too often.

"When anxious, we can feel so overwhelmed we need to be heard right then and there," says Melissa Kester, LFMT, a marriage and family therapist. "However, what we share is a very chaotic speech with everything plus the kitchen sink. While we are monologuing hoping desperately to be heard, our partner [might tune] us out." There are so many other ways you can avoid falling into this habit. You could go to the gym, run, call a friend, or leave everything with a therapist— anything that will save your relationship.

10. Constantly Doubting the Relationship

When you constantly doubt the commitment of your partner or the safety of your relationship, it can help to step back and see if your suspicions are due to anxiety.

"People with anxiety have negative self-talk, which can make them not trust that they are loved," says Tina B. Tessina, Ph.D., psychotherapist, and author of *Dr. Romance's Guide to Finding Love Today.* "This doubt can frustrate a partner, and eventually cause them to give up on the relationship." To do whatever you can to reinvigorate everything is important, not only for your tranquility, but also for your partner.

11. Getting Super-Angry

"Anger can come when we are feeling panicked, trapped, and unheard," says Kester. "When we share something important or try to stop feeling bad, our brain flips, our primitive self kicks in, we will experience blackouts, lose control of ourselves, and lose oral skills."

However, there are many healthier ways to get those thoughts out, or more importantly, to stop them altogether. Therapy can be a great place to start, as can the above-described changes in lifestyle.

12. Making Small Problems Big

If you have anxiety, you may have a breakdown over small things that would not usually bother you. As Sedacca says, "Anxious partners tend to catastrophize situations, blowing things up to mean more or appear more threatening than they really are." This is another side effect of anxiety and can be handled through therapy.

13. Avoiding Conflict at all Costs

One of the more unproductive things that happen in a relationship is to shut down. Yet, that is what tends to happen when you battle anxiety.

"People who tend to be more anxious tend to think disagreements are a bad thing," says life coach, Elizabeth Su. "We are often people-pleasers and worry that if we have a disagreement with our partner, it means our relationship is doomed." Anxiety makes it difficult to see that arguments are actually a good thing. Don't try to prevent your anxiety from engaging in productive conversations.

ANXIETY IN RELATIONSHIPS
THERESA WILLIAMS

CHAPTER 8

"Fear of abandonment and how can be treated"

Chapter 8: Fear of Abandonment and How It Can Be Treated

Fear of abandonment is the overriding fear that people will leave near you. Everyone can develop a fear of giving up. It can be deeply rooted in your traumatic experience as a child or in adult depression.

When you fear failure, maintaining healthy relationships can be almost impossible. The paralyzing fear will put you up against a wall to avoid being harmed, and you may be sabotaging relationships unintentionally.

The first step to overcoming anxiety is to understand why you feel the way you do. You can address your fears on your own or through professional therapy. However, fear of abandonment may also be part of a personality disorder requiring treatment.

Different Types of Fear of Abandonment

You may fear that someone you love will physically leave you and not come back. There are many examples of abandonment fear. You might be afraid that someone will give up on your emotional needs. You may be able to maintain yourself through ties with a parent, partner, or friend.

Fear of Emotional Abandonment

This kind of abandonment may be less noticeable, but it is no less painful. Emotional needs exist for all of us. When these conditions are not met, you may feel unrecognized, unloved, and disconnected. You may feel very much alone, even if you are in a relationship with a physically present person.

If you have undergone emotional renunciation in the past, especially as a child, you may be constantly fearful that it will happen again.

Fear of Abandonment in Children

It is normal for babies and children to experience a period of separation fear. A child may scream, yell, or refuse to let go if a parent or caregiver is leaving them. At this stage, children have difficulty understanding when or if the person will return.

As they begin to understand that the parent does come back, the child resolves their terror. This happens to most children by their third birthday.

Abandonment Anxiety in Relationships

You can be afraid of allowing yourself to be insecure in a relationship. You may have problems with confidence and worry about your relationship too much. That can make your partner suspicious.

Symptoms of the Fears of Abandonment

When you fear abandonment, you can likely identify some of these signs and symptoms:

- Overly sensitive to criticism

- Trouble trusting in others

- Difficulty making friends, unless you are sure you want them

- Taking extreme measures to prevent rejection or separation

- Patterns of unhealthy relationships

- Staying in a relationship even to the point that it is not healthy for you

- Blaming yourself when things don't work out

- Trouble committing to a relationship

- Working too hard to please people

- Getting attached to people quickly and moving on too quickly

Causes of Abandonment

Abandonment problems in relationships may be due to having been emotionally or physically abandoned in the past.

For example:

- For a child, a parent or caregiver may be absent or dead.

- Parental negligence may have been felt.

- Your colleagues might have rejected you.

- You have suffered through a loved one's chronic illness.

- A romantic partner may have suddenly left you or been

unfaithful.

These events can lead to a fear of abandonment.

Avoidant Personality Disorder

An avoidant personality disorder is a personality disorder that may include anxiety and a socially depressed or deficient sense of abandonment.

Separation Anxiety Disorder

If a child does not resolve separation anxiety issues, and it interferes with their daily work, a separation anxiety disorder can occur.

The Signs and Symptoms Include the Following:

- Panic attacks

- Depression with the thought of the separation of loved ones

- Refusal to leave home without a loved one, or fear of being alone

- Hallucinations with separation of loved ones

- Physical problems such as stomach pain or headache, when separated from loved ones

Long-Term Effects of Fear of Abandonment

The long-term effects of the fear of giving up may include:

- Challenging connections with friends and romantic partners

- Poor self-esteem

- Issues with self-confidence

- Mood swings

- Codependence

- Depression

- Fear of intimacy

- Panic problems

Examples of Fear of Abandonment

Here are a few examples of what the fear of abandonment may look like:

With the longer-term effects of fear of abandonment, you may think, "No connection, no drop."

- You are obsessively worried about your perceived flaws and what others might think about you.

- You are always the most pleasant person. You don't want to give any reason that someone doesn't want you to stay.

- You are crushed when someone criticizes you or gets upset with you in any way.

- When you feel slighted, you overreact.

- You feel insufficient and unattractive.

- Even if the other person asks for space, you are clingy.

- You are often jealous, suspicious of your partner, or critical of him.

Fear of abandonment is not a diagnosed mental health disorder, but it can certainly be detected and discussed to ease the effects. Diagnosing fear of abandonment and fear of rejection may also be part of a diagnosable personality disorder or other condition to be treated.

Recovery Problems

Once you know that you fear loss, you can do some things to start on your road to recovery.

Remove some slackness and stop making harsh judgments on yourself. Think about all the positive qualities that make you a good partner and mate.

Speak to the other person and discuss how your fear of abandonment came to be. Be aware of what you deserve from others. Explain where you are coming from, but don't create something dramatic to fix your fear of abandonment. Don't expect or ask more than is fair of them.

Work to maintain friendships and build a support network. Strong friendships will strengthen your sense of belonging and self-worth.

If this is not practical, consider talking to a qualified therapist. You will benefit from individual advice.

How to Assist Someone with Abandonment Problems

Some strategies to try if someone you know is dealing with a fear of abandonment:

- Begin the conversation. Encourage them to speak, but don't press them too much.

- Understand that the fear is real for them, whether it makes sense to you or not.

- Make sure you're committed to them and not going to abandon them just when they start to trust and confide in you.

- Ask what you can do to assist whenever possible.

- Suggest treatment, but don't push it on them. If you want to start, offer your help in finding a professional therapist. Let them guide the process as they feel comfortable with it.

10 Habits That Can Make Your Partner's Anxiety Worse

As the partner of an anxious person, you can play a critical role in alleviating the symptoms of their condition and making life for them (and you) easier. As we have seen, there many different types of anxiousness that have historically been characterized as anxiety disorders. If we think of anxiety as an emotion characterized by excessive worry or fear, then we can understand the common thread that often runs through anxiety disorders. We have also seen that some conditions characterized by worry or fear like post-traumatic stress disorder have recently been redefined by psychiatrists (at least in the United States) and may technically be seen today as "anxiety disorders." Anxiety is a common thread in many dysfunctional ways of thinking or behavior patterns and keeping this in mind is an important step that can lead to change.

Regardless of the type of worry your partner faces, you can be of help to them by helping them avoid habits that can make their symptoms worse. These are habits that you can work into your own life to steer you away from developing anxiety yourself. They will give you an opportunity to help you interact better with the anxious person in your life. By recognizing these dysfunctional habits, you can minimize the impact of your partner's anxiousness and help place your relationship on the road toward being worry-free.

Habit 1: Setting Unattainable Goals

The first habit that will certainly make your partner's anxiety symptoms worse is setting unattainable goals. This is a habit that the partner might also develop. It can prove unhealthy in your anxiety-fraught relationship. By setting impossible goals, the anxious person sets themselves up for a whirlwind of emotions that includes worry, fear, and anger. These emotions come from a subconscious realization that the goal may be beyond their reach, resulting in time spent worrying about the outcome. These emotions stem from the whole gamut of emotions that ensue when the goal inevitably fails.

As we have seen, anxious people can have intense reactions to things that may not disturb others. Having a plan or a goal fail (especially if it is an important one) can be devastating to anybody, even without a mental health issue, so it is not difficult to see why this would be a problem. By setting a reasonable, attainable goal, you and your partner can reduce the anxiousness that comes with reaching for something that cannot be achieved, and then having to deal with the consequences that inevitably come along.

Habit 2: Unhealthy Dietary Habits (Such as Excessive Smoking or Alcohol Consumption)

This is a common habit that an anxious person can drop (although it may be easier for some people than others.) It may come as a surprise to some those certain foods or substances can exacerbate worry. There are several products that should be avoided, but the big ones are caffeinated products like coffee and energy drinks, alcoholic beverages, and tobacco-containing products. Do you think it's a good idea to give your partner, who stays up all night worrying about things, an energy drink, or a big pot of coffee a few hours before bedtime? Avoiding these substances will help keep their anxiety from getting worse and maintain your sanity.

Habit 3: Excessive Use of social media

We live in an age of social media addiction, and many people do not have a full understanding of just how problematic this can be. Anxious people tend to obsess over things or blow things out of proportion. When you consider that much of the information that comes from news programs or is posted to social media is exaggerated, designed to inflame the reader, or is outright untrue, it should be obvious why social media can be a problem.

It is a good idea to steer your partner away from using social media if you can. It is also a good idea for you to avoid using social platforms in front of them (or at all.) Another part of this is avoiding using forms of communication other than face-to-face. By limiting your conversation to standard, old-fashioned face-to-face communication, you can prevent the worries and fears that come from unclear or misinterpreted messages that are usually more dramatic than necessary.

Habit 4: Depriving Yourself of Sleep

Sleep deprivation can exacerbate the condition of someone dealing with mental health concerns. This is true for anxiety, as well as other conditions like depression, bipolar disorder, and the like. The idea here is that the brain needs sleep to function normally and to maintain the body in homeostasis. Scientists and mental health professionals are currently engaged in an active debate as to precisely why sleep is so important, especially concerning the value of sleep-in individuals with mental health concerns. Do yourself and your partner a favor and try not to deprive them of sleep. Encourage them to get about eight hours each night and see how it affects their level of anxiety.

Habit 5: Not Getting Enough Exercise

Exercise is not only important in keeping your body in tiptop shape, but it also releases endorphins that cause people to feel happy and energetic. Indeed, it has been argued that the sedentary lifestyle of modern people has affected us in several negative and problematic ways, and the impact that being sedentary can have on the mind is often overlooked. You can help your significant other reduce their anxiety by encouraging them to exercise and by making sure that you are not the cause of why they are not getting enough exercise.

Habit 6: Not Being Honest About How You Are Feeling

A habit that anxious people share with depressed people is that sometimes they are not honest about how they are feeling. They may say that they are fine, when in reality; they are feeling down in the dumps or are worried about something. You can help your partner avoid this habit and combat their anxiety by informing them that how they feel matters to you and that it is important to you that they are honest. You cannot help an anxious or depressed person feel better if you do not know how they truly feel.

Habit 7: Magnifying a Situation (Blowing Things Out of Proportion)

Anxious and depressed people tend to engage in something called catastrophizing. This is also called magnifying, and it refers to blowing matters out of proportion in a dysfunctional way. Anxious people do not necessarily do this on purpose. Because they tend to over-worry or obsess about things, they can attach more importance to things than what is there. Helping your partner drop the habit of magnifying or catastrophizing is an important step in the process of salvaging or maintaining your relationship.

Habit 8: Not Listening

This is a habit that anxious individuals and their partners can be guilty of on a regular basis. Although, an anxious person may hang onto your every word and *hear* you, are they listening? Remember that anxiety-fraught individuals can misinterpret or misunderstand ambiguous words or communicated information (via text, email, etc.). Listening, therefore, becomes a very critical skill to have in a relationship where anxiety is an issue. Drop the habit of not listening to one another, and both of you will see all the ways that your relationship can be improved.

Habit 9: Allowing Your Partner to Isolate Themselves

Depressed or anxious individuals can isolate themselves. In depressed individuals, this can be attributed to chemical signals that cause a host of symptoms that lead to them becoming more withdrawn, while in anxious persons, it may be due to avoiding situations that trigger their worries, obsessions, or compulsions. Isolating yourself is a habit that anxious people will have to drop if they hope to get better, and as their partner, you will be making a big difference if you can help them.

Habit 10: Managing Stress Poorly, both Inside and Outside a Relationship

It can be argued that anxious people, by definition, have difficulty managing stress, but managing stress is important in any relationship whether there is anxiety or not. Think about a relationship where both partners work or have busy schedules. You want to make sure that you both have time for the things that you enjoy and that you have ways of diffusing anger-fraught or stressful situations. An inability to manage stress can be a bad habit in any relationship, but in relationships where one partner is anxious, this habit can result in a catastrophe. Do yourself a favor and talk to your partner about how the two of you will handle situations that stress you out.

Building Trust in a Relationship in a Beautiful Way

Trust is perhaps the most fundamental and essential element in a successful relationship. Only when we can trust our partner fully and they can trust us, are we truly able to be safe and happy. The following suggestions will help you identify whether your relationship is good and how your relationship can be successful if it is not. These seven steps will help build confidence in your relationship.

Consistency is the first thing to look for. In your relationship, how honest are you? Your partner, how about it? Can you count on each other? Are you there for each other every day? Romance and excitement are beautiful concepts, but daily routine and reasonable standards lead to a sense of security. Being reliable every day will build a trust-based relationship.

The next thing you have to be careful about is **communication** skills. How well do you send and receive the intended messages for each other? Do your words correspond to your facial expressions? Does your body language suit what you are saying? Is your intended message sent? Many contradictions in a relationship are the result of a misunderstanding. This is usually a communication malfunction at the base. You and your partner must be able to trust each other's words, to be sure of what is said and what is intended. If your words suit your body language, you can build confidence in a relationship.

Belief in yourself, belief in your partner, and the competence of each other as people is essential to a trusting relationship. If your partner has issues with which you are not confident, a gentle and frank discussion on your insecurities is much better than silence, anger, and frustration to build a relationship of confidence. Seeing the qualities of your partner and then feeling complimented and appreciated creates a feeling of comfort and acceptance. This will come back to you in the end. If your partner does anything that you don't like or are unable to do, a caring and supportive conversation will become the foundation of a loving and trusting relationship, although it is sometimes challenging.

In any successful relationship, complete **honesty** is imperative. The fourth step you will take is to learn how to be loyal to your partner. You can't build confidence in a relationship if you keep secrets. Any kind of secrecy will kill the trust in a relationship. It may seem simple and straightforward to be honest and open, but it takes purpose. The truth is always revealed, and the truth always frees you. Keeping a secret puts a barrier between you and your partner. Secrets need energy to continue and more lies to maintain as time goes on. This is time and energy that you should put into your relationship in a positive way. Regardless of how difficult it seems; an honest and open relationship is always a trustworthy one.

As mentioned, good communication is a necessary part of building confidence in a relationship. The fifth step, **sharing**, brings your needs to the next level. It can be uncomfortable, especially early in a relationship, to share your needs. Yet, we find a way to meet our needs, whether we communicate them or not and it is often unhealthy. To maintain a solid relationship and build confidence, your physical, emotional, and social needs need to be shared with your partner. You must also be willing to hear them and try to meet the needs of your partner. Having your girlfriend or boyfriend feel what you need, or what upsets you, creates tension and frustration in building trust. Expressing your desires doesn't make you selfish, but self-aware, and you can trust your partner a great deal.

Learn to **say no**. It is human to like people and want to please them, but if you put the needs of others first every time, it can have a negative effect on you. He/she must know what you're saying. It's a good thing if your partner expresses his wishes, but you don't have to say yes to everything. Say no when you need to make your partner see who you are and appreciate you when you set limits. If you never say no, they will not respect you. Standing down and seeing your partner do the same creates a climate of giving and taking, when appropriate, and helps build trust in the relationship.

All about you. As a human being, you must always **continue to grow** and extend. Anything living requires constant care and attention and continues to grow and change. By continuously improving yourself and allowing your partner to do the same, you will become two stronger halves of your relationship. You must also maintain the relationship constantly as your own living being apart from both of you. Like a river, sometimes the water slows down and becomes dull. As well, it enlarges and goes faster, and the bottom vanishes. Eventually, the river is narrow and chaotic to maintain. The water flows across rocks and drops down the cascades. Your bond will be the same, and while the rough sections can be painful, after a waterfall, the cleanest water comes. Recognizing and coping with these facets of a relationship can build trust in your relationship.

For you to have good, happy, affectionate, pleasant relationships it is essential to understand forgiveness and confidence in relationships.

Other relationships are shallower, like the person with whom you speak while shopping at the grocery store or people you see only in church on Sundays. Some connections are more profound, like good neighbors and your hairdresser. Many relationships are much more complex, such as partner, parents, kids, grandchildren, close friends, etc. That relationship, regardless of its degree, is affected by our choices. Somebody has been hurt when you made poor choices in your life. We will never harm ourselves if we say something bad, neglect others, and choose to be dishonest, or go the wrong direction. Since everything we do affects someone else, relationships can be very tense and need reparation. This is one of my favorite topics because I have been through the restoration of relationships that I didn't think could ever be good again.

I have had the personal experience of witnessing the magic of recoupling relationships with the people I love most on earth. It is possible that a relationship cannot be remedied because the other person has no desire to work with you on it. However, it is completely possible to resolve even the worst situations. Don't give up hope.

One goal in managing relationships is to know that you are unable to take over the other person. If you hurt somebody, make modifications; don't apologize and make modifications. Don't try to justify what you have done, focus on how to make modifications. This is the right thing to do, and it is the thing that keeps you aware that you are doing what you can to restore the relationship, to the extent that it depends on you.

Responsibility. You have no power over whether the other party wants to accept the modifications but recognize that it does not mean that you accept their apology. This means that you take 100% responsibility for who you are in the relationship. These two things are very different. You need to understand and accept the disparity in the two for you to have healthy ties. The other person must come to the position of reconciliation and obligation on their own. You could choose to not forgive them or trust them again. They could choose not to forgive you. Often, when they see consistent, honest perseverance in your actions, they will forgive and trust you. In the relationships you have, you are responsible for you. This also refers to the other person; they are liable for their part in the relationship.

Forgiveness and confidence are two of the toughest things in relationships. Forgiveness does not depend on faith, but trust depends very much on forgiveness. If someone hasn't forgiven you, they probably won't allow you to earn their trust. Somebody can forgive you, but they may never trust you again. Whether or not they choose to trust you again is beyond your control. You're going to live in a constant loop of chaos if you try to control what can only be in their judgment.

As an act of humility, we forgive others. Matthew 18:21-22 says: Then Peter came to him and said, "God, how much longer shall my brother sin against me and I forgive him? Up until to seven times?" Jesus said to him, "I do not say seven times to you, but until seventy times seven." This doesn't mean it will be easy, and it can be almost impossible in some situations in our humanity. If we invoke the strength and courage of the Almighty, the "impossible" is fully possible.

Confidence, on the other hand, is something people have to win within themselves. Many, many scriptures talk of believing in the Lord. Psalm 40:4 says: "How satisfied is the man who has made the Lord his faith and has not turned to the arrogant or the deceiving." I love this verse because Our God loves us so much that He would never hurt us by orgy or error, but by men..

How to Break the Cycle of Anxiety

Anxiety is described as the act of having a persistent and excessive worry. However, the issue with anxiety goes far beyond a single worry. If an individual were to be dealing with only one worry, then it probably would not seem like as big of a deal. Unfortunately, people who have anxiety disorders, more specifically generalized anxiety disorder, tend to be swarmed by one worry that then leads to another worry, then another, and so on. This explains why anxiety is a cycle.

Worries are also what keep that cycle going round and round. Even though a person might be experiencing a worry that could be solved, the worry continues for multiple reasons. The first reason is that some worries can fall under the category of biased thinking. This could mean an individual is giving too much weight to the likelihood that a negative outcome will take place. Biased thinking can also mean a person is exaggerating how bad the negative outcome will end up being.

Some types of worries are strengthened by the negative thoughts that a person has about themselves like the person is not capable of coping with any type of negative outcome that could occur.

The second reason a person might find their worries continuing to take up most of their thoughts is that some worries persist due to how certain information in the environment is processed. Someone who suffers from generalized anxiety disorder will sometimes selectively choose to investigate the information that will support their worries while ignoring any information that refutes their worrying thoughts.

Memories can also be selective, just like a person's worries. In some instances, people who have issues with anxiety have a difficult time remembering any data that portrays a contradiction to the worry they are currently dealing with.

The third possible reason why an individual's worries might be persistent is based on how the person is responding to those worries. Someone who has an untreated anxiety disorder might respond to their fears by trying one of three things. They might attempt to suppress their worries, seek reassurance that nothing negative will happen, or they could end up avoiding a situation that triggers their fear.

The greatest downfall to choosing any of these responses is that any one of them will make a person feel horrible, which will lead to their worries being reinforced. This makes it extremely difficult to break the person's cycle of anxiety later.

However, with the right mindset and the use of some helpful changes in a person's thoughts and behaviors, someone can break their cycle of anxiety. A simple example of a negative thought can help to prepare people to begin the process of breaking the cycle of anxiety. The thought "I know that my boyfriend is going to break up with me" is an impulsive thought that is extremely normal for a person to have when they are in a relationship. The response could pertain to a particular situation that happens, or it could appear to come 'out of the blue.'

Even though that thought may be normal for a person to have, someone who suffers from extreme anxiety would give that thought too much weight and meaning. This ends up leading to the person mulling over all the possible reasons for why their thought could become true, as well as the person will try to lessen their anxiety in the short-term. Unfortunately, when a person tries to reduce their anxiety in the short-term, this only makes that same anxiety stronger in the long-term.

The belief, which in this case is that a person's boyfriend is going to break up with them, becomes that much more significant and has experienced a lot more regularly. The belief will also be much more intense than it would be for someone who does not have an anxiety problem.

The above points are some of the major reasons a person should investigate overcoming their anxiety by breaking the cycle of it. The first strategy for doing so is to learn how to accept that not everyone believes there is an actual reason to become worried. Not every thought that a person has is going to be true.

Rather than trying to battle with someone's negative beliefs, they should start focusing on acceptance-based techniques that involve a person identifying the negative thought they are having and putting a label on it. The label might be that the thought is a worry or a judgment. The person should also be trying to show mindfulness now when the belief first comes out as well as now when the belief begins to fade from the person's awareness.

It can be difficult and intimidating for a person to learn how to accept and alter a person's negative thoughts so they can be mindful of when the thoughts come up. It is for this reason that a person may want to consider looking into some support groups, either in person or online, that can help them work through the process.

The next strategy for breaking the cycle of anxiety is to begin asking the right questions. A person goes about doing so by severing the link between the biases created from their thoughts, as well as from the information they have gathered. The process that the person will take is called cognitive restructuring, which is the foundation for the treatment approach known as cognitive-behavioral therapy.

Cognitive restructuring allows an individual to critically evaluate any possible distorted thought they might be having. The thought "my boyfriend is going to break up with me" is considered a type of distorted thought. The cognitive restructuring comes into play when the individual begins asking themselves a series of questions about the belief that will result in a more balanced view of all the relevant facts a person needs to make their thoughts more rational.

The process of cognitive restructuring will take a bit of time, but the results will be worth it at the end. The first step to restructuring someone's thoughts is to learn how to notice when someone is having distorted thoughts. However, it is better to only focus on one type of cognitive distortion at a time. A few examples of distorted thoughts include mindreading, personalizing, underestimated coping abilities, catastrophizing, and entitlement beliefs.

For one week, an individual should focus on their distorted thoughts, like their entitlement beliefs. The person should look at any moments when they find themselves having those entitlement beliefs. For example, they may notice they are expecting their friends to pay for dinner, and so they do not offer to pay any amount towards the meal.

When the person realizes their cognitive distortion, they should then ask themselves what other ways they might think about the situation. Concerning the entitlement beliefs example, the person might ask themselves what other actions they could take, rather than not offering to pay their share at dinner. Three alternative questions that they could consider are: What is the worst possible thing that could happen if they simply offer to chip in some money? What is the best possible outcome that could occur if the person were to pay for their meal? And what is the most realistic outcome that will happen if they pay for their meal?

The second step to cognitive restructuring is for an individual to begin keeping track of how accurate their thoughts are. For example, a person could be thinking about how their problem will help them find a solution to said problem.

For example, a person could write down every time they notice that they are overthinking in one column, and then note whether the overthinking leads to any useful problem-solving in the second column.

When the end of the week comes around, the person should then determine what percentage of time their overthinking led them to conduct some useful problem-solving moments.

A person could also choose to record the estimated number of minutes they spent overthinking when they can take notice of when it occurred. This approach can allow a person to notice how many minutes of overthinking they did in succession with their useful problem-solving moments.

The third step for the process of cognitive restructuring is for a person to figure out a way to test their thoughts behaviorally. It could be that the person does not have any time to take a break. For one week, the person could go about following their typical routine, and by the end of each day, they will rate how productive they were based on a 0-10 scale.

During the second week, the individual is asked to take a five-minute break every hour. They are also asked to do the same rating at the end of each day that week. At the end of the second week, the person will look at the ratings for both week one and week two and compare their ratings of productivity for both weeks. The person will likely find that they were more productive when they took smaller breaks every 60 minutes.

The next step in the cognitive restructuring process is for an individual to evaluate all the evidence that strengthens and weakens a particular thought they are having. For example, if a person has a thought such as, "I will never be capable of getting this done right," they should consider all the evidence they have that would prove that statement to be true as well as all the information that can prove the statement is not true.

Like tracking the accuracy of someone's thoughts, the person can write down their objective evidence, which supports the thought that they cannot get something right in one column and put the objective evidence that supports the idea that their thought is not true in the second column.

Once the individual has done this, they would then want to write out a few balanced thoughts that would accurately reflect their evidence. An example of such a thought could be that the person is aware that they have made poor decisions in the past, but they have also made a lot of good decisions that led to their success.

It is okay for a person to not completely believe in their new thought that proves their original negative thought to be wrong. It is important to start experimenting with trying out thoughts that poke holes in their negative thinking.

Mindfulness meditation is the next step to cognitive restructuring. During this process, a person chooses a focus of attention, for example, their breathing. Then, for a certain number of minutes, the person will have to focus all their attention on the sensations they experience while they are breathing, rather than simply thinking about the fact that they are breathing.

ANXIETY IN RELATIONSHIPS
THERESA WILLIAMS

CHAPTER 9

"Personal tips for overcoming anxiety and live a happy relationship"

Chapter 9: Personal Tips for Overcoming Anxiety and Having a Happy Relationship

One of the most important things that the spouse or partner of an anxious person has to recognize is that their role is as a supporter. You know your significant other better than anyone else, but that still leaves the primary task of dealing with anxiousness on them rather than on you. This does not mean that you should ignore the anxious symptoms to eat away at the person until it irreparably damages their life. Still, your place in the big picture should be recognized by both of you.

The role of the supporter is an important one. Sure, sitting on the sidelines can be frustrating sometimes, but a solid supporter is just what your partner or spouse needs right now. If you are the one dealing with anxiousness, then these tips will help you get an understanding of the sorts of things that your partner can do for you.

Tip 1: Understand that overcoming anxiety is a process

(Anxiety is not something that someone will just snap out of.)

Anxiety is not like having a common cold. It is not something that you get and can find a resolution with the snap of a finger. Anxiety disorders should be thought of as conditions that require treatment. What this means for the significant other of an anxious person is that you should be realistic about your partner's anxiety. They are not going to snap out of their anxiety, and it is more than a little unfair of you to expect them to. As a supporter of an anxious person, it is critical to recognize that you will be helping them through the long process of overcoming their illness.

Tip 2: Be conscious of your dysfunctional thoughts or preconceived notions

Anxiousness is characterized by a cavalcade of dysfunctional thoughts that people often are not aware that they are having. Unfortunately, for the significant others of anxious persons, they can have a spiral of dysfunctional thoughts that can affect how they perceive and interact with their anxious partner. The meaning here is not that the partner is necessarily at risk for worry, but merely that the partner should recognize how notions can color their interaction with their partner that they have about their condition (including the subconscious stigma that men and women often have towards the conditions of the mind).

Tip 3: Provide reassurance that things are going to turn out all right

One of the most important things that you can do while supporting someone else through anxiety (or any condition) is to reassure that thing are going to turn out all right. This does not mean telling a lie. If someone has a terminal illness like stage IV cancer, it is important to recognize exactly what that means. Nevertheless, honest reassurance in the case of anxiousness is a little different. Anxiety can and does frequently get better, so reminding your partner of that can place a positive thought in their head that can be an important part of creating real change in their life.

Tip 4: Encourage your partner to get help

A difficult reality for partners of anxious people to accept is that it is not their job to steer their partner in the direction they think they should go. We have established that anxiety disorders are conditions that typically do not get better without treatment, but that does not mean that it is your role as their supporter to force them to get treatment or dictate what form of treatment they need.

Intervention-type maneuvers can be problematic in mental health. This is especially true in the case of anxiousness, where the individual may already be inclined to have a suspicious or fearful approach to others or the world in general. Coercing an anxious partner into treatment is not a good idea. What you can do is educate yourself about the help that is available for their condition and encourage them to get help. That is all that you can do.

Tip 5: Be patient as your significant other moves through their condition

It is important to be patient when dealing with a person with a mental health condition, which is just as true for anxiety as other conditions like depression. Recall that anxiety disorders include conditions as divergent as GAD, specific phobias, and obsessive-compulsive disorder. The point here is that some of these conditions can be very debilitating for the individual dealing with and very frustrating for the partner or family member around it. For your sanity (and for your partner), it is important to be patient. The change will happen slowly, and it will help you to keep this in mind.

Tip 6: Provide ongoing education and support to your partner

Being supportive means being someone that your significant other can go to when they need help. Again, the goal here is not to force your partner to do something that they may not be ready to do, but to support them as they decide to make a change and take steps towards making that change. As a supportive partner, you can provide ongoing education for yourself about anxiety and related conditions like depression and you can even find ways to pass this information along to your partner.

Anxious individuals can have exaggerated or otherwise excessive or unnecessary reactions to stimuli, so it is important that you and your partner both recognize that you are occupying a supportive role. If your partner feels that you are attempting to manipulate them or push them in a particular direction, they may begin to mistrust you and avoid you. Therefore, it is important to approach your partner's anxiety from the standpoint of educating both of you on this subject.

Tip 7: Recognize that no one understands your partner's anxiety more than your partner does

As much as you may educate yourself about anxiousness, no one is better poised to understand your partner's anxiety than them. Sure, you may be around them for several hours of the day. You may feel that you see aspects of their anxiety that they appear to be unconscious of. Because you are not experiencing what they are and are not inside their head to know what the triggers are, perhaps you do not understand their condition as well as you might think. Use this as an opportunity to let your partner educate you about their worries, not the other way around.

Tip 8: Be available, not overbearing

It is easy to fall into the trap of being overbearing when you are in a relationship and notice that your partner needs help with something. You may find that you have an overweening desire to help them, and perhaps you feel that you can see matters from a vantage point that they may not see. Even if that is the case, your partner does not have the ability to make decisions for themselves. Loved one or not, you do not necessarily have the right to force them to do what you want if they are not a danger to themselves or others. If you are interested in maintaining a loving relationship with your significant other, you should focus on being available and supporting rather than overbearing.

Tip 9: Take your partner's comments seriously

One of the ways that you learn the character of your partner's anxiousness (and gain a deep sense of what they are going through) is by talking to them. Your partner's anxiety is just that, their anxiety, and you need to leave it to them to clue you in on how they are feeling and why. Therefore, it is important as a supportive partner to talk to your partner and exercise active listening. Just as your anxious partner may hang on to your every word, you need to learn to pay attention to your partner's words. When your partner tells you something about themselves or what they are going through, take it seriously.

Tip 10: Remember that empathy is important

Sympathy is a word that many people understand, although they do not always show it. Sympathy involves feeling compassion and tolerance for others, a feeling that comes from a deep understanding of where the other person is coming from. We can show sympathy for others through our words, actions, or even by our facial expressions.

However, empathy is something different. Empathy involves sharing the feelings of others: experiencing what they are experiencing. Although having true empathy for someone with a mental condition may be fraught with danger, this is something that many partners can do, and their relationships can be improved through it.

Having empathy for your partner means that you recognize that their anxiety is not just an illness that they are dealing with, but it may be part of them. They may have dealt with anxiousness in some way or another for most of their life, and they may not understand how to live without their anxious, obsessive, or compulsive behaviors. By truly coming to experience the world the way they do, you can be a real supporter—someone who can deal with their highs and lows right along with them.

Setting a Goal for a Healthy Relationship

For relationships to succeed, like in every area of life, you need to know what you want. While, out of dumb luck, you can come upon a successful relationship, it helps to be clear about your target. This clarification can be used to point you in the generally correct direction and guide you along the way.

What makes for a stable bond in childhood always makes for a safe adult relationship. So, you should think of relationships as having the following three basic characteristics:

Emotional availability: Children need to be physically and emotionally close to their parents to make them feel safe, but adult relationships are more dependent on emotionally close partners. Although separations and romantic long-distance relationships can trigger a strain, they are not necessarily deal-breakers. Partners must accept each other's needs and be responsive to them. When your partner remains emotionally distant or aggressive, you are likely to feel isolated, ignored, or discarded, and you may doubt your worth as an individual.

Secure haven: Just as a child runs back to his mother when threatened or upset, partners in a stable relationship turn to each other in times of difficulty when they need reassurance or support. Since life often requires at least some pain and fatiguing challenges, it is vital to have a partner who is willing to provide support, aid, and relief from those problems. The problems of life are less overcome by people who know they have this trustworthy "bridge in a storm." Unfortunately, if your partner dismisses or criticizes you, then you will not turn to him; or if you turn to him, you will eventually feel insulted.

Secure basis: To feel fulfilled in life and truly loved in a relationship, people need to be able to pursue the desires of their hearts—or just be able to explore what those desires might be. Both partners promote and support these activities in healthy relationships.

When you think about the attributes of a healthy relationship, note that to build them, all partners must work together. Partners have to be in agreement and agree that it is necessary for emotional availability. Security and relaxation provide a safe refuge in times of trouble. Proper support makes the relationship a stable base from which to explore the world. While you are probably more worried about a partner being able to give you these "gifts," it is equally vital for him to be able to accept them as an open reciprocal give-and-take nurtures the relationship. In the same way, you need to be able to give and receive these items.

What to Look for in a Partner

The person best qualified to be there for you in this way, technically speaking, has the attributes mentioned below. I offer this with the qualification that someone whose characteristics do not match everything on this list could still satisfy your needs. This is intended only as a rough guideline—as something to consider (though seriously) while you are looking for a new partner or evaluating how well the person beside you is meeting your needs. This being the case, you want a partner who is:

Securely attached and mature: Since these people are confident with themselves and their relationships, they can be emotionally intimate, as well as continuing to pursue independent, personal interests with themselves and with their partners. We are also able to talk about themselves and their lives in a way that is accessible, reflective, and emotionally linked. This allows them to recognize their limitations and to admit their mistakes in a non-defensive manner—all without sacrificing their positive sense of self. Understanding that other people are similarly flawed, they will quickly forgive their spouses.

A successful communicator: This type of partner is excellent at listening and communicating, which allows them to nurture and maintain close relations. They are also able to work together through disputes. They have these skills in part because they are inherently excellent at detecting and controlling their emotions—a definite bonus when you attempt to communicate and work through the challenges that naturally occurs in an emotionally intimate relationship.

Appreciative of you: Falling in love is not enough. Since relationships are co-created, they will only make you happy in the long term if your partner loves you and supports you—and works in a way to express this. You need to give your partner interest in getting to know you. While it is at first a steep learning curve, the journey to know you better should never plateau. You will always be happier with the guidance and motivation to pursue your interests and achieve your full potential.

A good fit: Enjoying time together is crucial. This means having at least some shared interests. Yet, it also means doing things together, even if this includes participating in conversations. Sharing each other's values, or at least honoring them, is very important for a long-term relationship. The more things that influence those ideals in everyday life, the more critical it is to share them. For example, when one partner is ready to have children, and the other partner is entirely against it, catastrophe awaits.

Ready for a relationship: Each partner must be able to pursue the relationship. This means devoting time and paying attention to it, both when you are together physically and when you are apart.

Again, it's important to note that you don't have to find Mr. or Ms. Perfect—which is fine because none of those people exist. You don't even need to consider Mr. or Ms. Perfect-For-Me. It will prove to be an endless search, hoping to find a better person just around the corner. What you need is to consider Mr. or Ms. Good-For-Me, instead. I'm not suggesting you settle for someone you're not happy with, but make sure you have your priorities straight. For that stable base, you're going to be able to tolerate a little mess, minimal interest in scaling a corporate ladder, or any other "fault" much easier. For example, less than motivated career ambitions represent the importance of relationships and other non-material aspects of life that your partner places upon.

One final caution: Don't be too quick to push past a date "nice-but-boring."

Nurturing a Relationship, You Feel Secure in

It can be completely fun to watch couples dance together. Watching two people flow in perfectly timed motions is fascinating. Some magnetic force apparently connects those that are most successful.

You'll want to nurture a relationship after finding a romantic partner, which can feel like that perfectly coordinated dance at its best. The two of you would work well together in such a relationship, communicate effectively, and trust each other, all while being in tune with each other. You would still want that to be a coordinated effort, even at its worst. Find ways to accept and work with any differences among yourselves, instead of trying to force each other to change.

Part of the beauty of enjoying such a supportive relationship is that it helps you feel more secure within yourself and your relationship.

Self-Disclosure

Your initial experience with a potential partner sets the stage for how your relationship story will unfold. It will go most smoothly at the beginning if the two of you open in synchrony with each other. One of you shares something personal, and the other one responds with empathy, sympathy, and disclosure of a similar nature. You both feel more energetic, and you are motivated to share more, to deepen the level of openness. You also develop a sense of security and faith in each other's company as you enjoy those intimate moments. The love and fondness that naturally emerges from these relationships is necessary to sustain a healthy long-term relationship.

If you have an insecure attachment style, getting to know each other with this kind of give-and-take probably won't go smoothly. For example, you may hope that expressing many of your problems at once would gain your partner's attention, comfort, and reassurance. On the other hand, the need for closeness may make you feel too vulnerable to share; so then, you may stay away, or you may stay nearby. You risk shutting your partner off in both situations. This often interferes with getting to know her and feeling empathy for her, as your attention is on whether your partner can support or hurt you.

If your relationships have been disrupted by the way you choose to communicate, perhaps it is time you approach it differently. Start by thinking about your motives. Keep an eye on when and how you share when you go forward.

You will want to share your personal experiences with your partner at the right time, as a way of getting closer and helping him or her understand you. As tempting as it may be to "unpack all your luggage" and share everything in detail, be mindful of what you are sharing. In general, share enough to understand your partner so that she can be empathetic and supportive. The rest will come out with time if you so choose.

For example, you might confess, "I'm worried about letting my guard down because my last girlfriend was critical of me all the time." By deciding not to say anything about it for the moment, you may keep your focus on your current relationship. You allow this prospective girlfriend to talk about herself or inquire about you more. She might say, "I know how you feel...." Or she might ask you, "What do you mean?" This way, you can direct your discoveries and a growing sense of connection to happen synchronously with your partner—leading to a sense of warmth and love that will ideally tide you over the years.

Conclusion

Anxiousness does not have to derail your life or the life of your partner. If you are in a relationship where anxiety is an issue, you should take comfort in knowing that anxiety symptoms can be managed effectively in various ways, relieving the hold that anxious thoughts have on your relationship. Part of what makes anxiousness so challenging to manage in relationships is that many people do not have an accurate understanding of what anxiety is, rendering the simple act of recognizing it a difficult one.

Perhaps the most well-known anxiety disorder is what psychologists refer to as generalized anxiety disorder. This is the disorder that most people are referring to when they talk about anxiety. However, it is estimated to account for slightly less than fifty percent of all cases of anxiety. A common category of disorders characterized by anxiety is specific phobias. Specific phobias are associated with excessive fear around a specific object or trigger, like crowds, spiders, or speaking publicly.

The first step to successfully dealing with anxiety in a relationship setting is to educate yourself enough on the subject so that you can understand the condition and all the way that it may surface in the relationship. This allows you not only to approach the anxiety in your relationship from the standpoint of knowledge, but it also permits you to show sympathy for your partner's anxiety because you understand it better and have an idea of where it may be coming from.

Being fully educated about worry requires that you have a basic understanding of anxiety disorders. Although many relationships are characterized by the type of anxiety that is associated with generalized anxiety disorder, other conditions like panic disorder, specific phobias, obsessive-compulsive disorder, or post-traumatic stress disorder, have different symptoms, which makes dealing with them a unique ordeal. The goal is not necessarily that the reader should know how each disorder should be managed, but to be able to recognize what type of anxiety their partner suffers from and to be aware that different types of anxiousness should be managed differently.

The question of where anxiety comes from is a loaded one. Although it has been observed that this condition does frequently run-in families, it has also been found that anxiety appears to be more common in Western countries than in developing countries (in addition to other notable demographic trends.) A potentially important cause of anxiety is the dysfunctional relationships that some people experience in their youth. This is the idea behind attachment theory: the model that shows how children learn how to interact with other people and their environment based on the relationship they have with their primary caregiver.

Anxiety can be treated successfully, providing relief for the millions of men and women that deal with anxiousness. Anxiety symptoms can be treated with medication, but it can also be treated successfully with therapy, dietary changes, and natural remedies. These natural remedies include things like herbs found in the environment, inositol, and transcendental meditation. Although, more research has to be done to show how effective these treatments are, they represent another option for people looking for alternatives to the more common medication and therapeutic options.

This would not be practical about dealing with anxiousness in relationships if it did not provide the reader with tips, they can follow to help them maintain their relationship in the face of worry. It is not easy dealing with anxiousness, either as the individual suffering from it or as the partner of the anxious individual, and this is a concept that recognizes this.

An important fact to know about anxiety is that it usually does not go away on its own. If anxiety is left untreated, it will persist, potentially derailing the anxious individual's familial and romantic relationships and preventing them from forming new enduring ones. The goal is to help the partner of the anxious person become more supportive, which may be so crucial for that person that it can change the course of their life. Anxiety can be beaten, but it will take effort. Reading this book was the first step in accomplishing this important work.